Handbook of Biopharma Industry Acronyms & Terms

The Acronyms, Terms, and Phrases for the Science and Business of the Pharmaceutical and Biotechnology Industries

Author and Editor:

Ronald P. Evens, PharmD, FCCP
CEO and President, M.A.P.S. 4 Biotec, Inc.
Clinical Professor, University of Florida, Jacksonville

Editorial Board:

Stephen Carroll, PhD
President, Altair Consulting
Previously, Vice-President, Scientific and
Product Development at Xoma LLC

Joel Covinsky, PharmD, FCCP
Consultant, Research and Development,
Pharmaceutical Industry
Previously, Vice-President Global Drug Development at Aventis

Edward F. Kenney, MS
Biopharmaceutical Consultant to CEO, Onyx Pharmaceuticals
Previously, Executive Vice-President and Chief Business
Officer at Onyx Pharmaceuticals

W0234801

JONES AND BARTLETT PUBLISHERS
Sudbury, Massachusetts
BOSTON   TORONTO   LONDON   SINGAPORE

World Headquarters
Jones and Bartlett Publishers
40 Tall Pine Drive
Sudbury, MA 01776
978-443-5000
info@jbpub.com
www.jbpub.com

Jones and Bartlett Publishers International
Barb House, Barb Mews
London W6 7PA
UNITED KINGDOM

Jones and Bartlett Publishers Canada
6339 Ormindale Way
Mississauga, Ontario L5V 1J2
CANADA

Jones and Bartlett's books and products are available through most bookstores and online book-sellers. To contact Jones and Bartlett Publishers directly, call 800-832-0034, fax 978-443-8000, or visit our website, www.jbpub.com.

Substantial discounts on bulk quantities of Jones and Bartlett's publications are available to corporations, professional associations, and other qualified organizations. For details and specific discount information, contact the special sales department at Jones and Bartlett via the above contact information or send an email to specialsales@jbpub.com.

The authors, editor, and publisher have made every effort to provide accurate information. However, they are not responsible for errors, omissions, or for any outcomes related to the use of the contents of this book and take no responsibility for the use of the products and procedures described. Treatments and side effects described in this book may not be applicable to all people; likewise, some people may require a dose or experience a side effect that is not described herein. Drugs and medical devices are discussed that may have limited availability controlled by the Food and Drug Administration (FDA) for use only in a research study or clinical trial. Research, clinical practice, and government regulations often change the accepted standard in this field. When consideration is being given to use of any drug in the clinical setting, the health care provider or reader is responsible for determining FDA status of the drug, reading the package insert, and reviewing prescribing information for the most up-to-date recommendations on dose, precautions, and contraindications, and determining the appropriate usage for the product. This is especially important in the case of drugs that are new or seldom used.

PRODUCTION CREDITS

Executive Publisher: Christopher Davis
Production Director: Amy Rose
Associate Editor: Kathy Richardson
Editorial Assistant: Jessica Acox
Production Assistant: Leah Corrigan
Manufacturing Buyer: Therese Connell

Associate Marketing Manager: Rebecca Wasley
Composition: Achorn International, Inc.
Cover Design: Kate Ternullo
Printing and Binding: Malloy, Inc.
Cover Printing: Malloy, Inc.
Cover Image: © Andrejs Pidjass/ShutterStock, Inc.

Library of Congress Cataloging-in-Publication Data

Evens, Ronald P.
  Handbook of biopharma industry acronyms and terms / Ronald P. Evens. — 1st ed.
    p. ; cm.
  ISBN-13: 978-0-7637-5296-5 (alk. paper)
  1. Drug development—Abbreviations. 2. Drug development—Acronyms. 3. Pharmaceutical industry Abbreviations. 4. Pharmaceutical industry—Acronyms. I. Title.
  [DNLM: 1. Drug Design—Abbreviations. 2. Drug Design—Handbooks. 3. Drug Industry—Abbreviations. 4. Drug Industry—Handbooks. 5. Pharmaceutical Preparations—Abbreviations. 6. Pharmaceutical Preparations—Handbooks. QV 13 E93h 2008]
  RS51.E94 2008
  615'.19—dc22

                                                                        2007042251
6048

Printed in the United States of America
12 11 10 09 08   10 9 8 7 6 5 4 3 2 1

CONTENTS

Overview and Introduction

Language can be either a facilitator or barrier to effective communication and is a cornerstone of any successful work environment, whether it is in research or business practices, or in collaborations between different types of workers, or even in an interpersonal relationship. In most of the world, languages are unique to each country, and cross-border collaboration requires translation and interpretation of words and phrases, along with their meanings and appropriate context. Ultimately, the learning of the other language itself is needed for fully effective communication.

Business worlds can also have their own language with distinct phrases and terms, based on the unique features of their technologies, science, products, employees, customers, and government relationships. The business worlds of home construction, agriculture, and space exploration are easy to recognize as unique from each other in technologies, products, and terminology. Certainly, the pharmaceutical and biotechnology industries (here-to-fore called the biopharma industry) have such special circumstances in at least seven areas: (1) their sophisticated and complex science base, (2) the medical practice and patient care context, (3) a research-intensive environment on at least four levels (basic laboratory, animal, clinical, and economic), (4) substantial government engagement and regulatory oversight, (5) highly varied and complex healthcare systems along with the related customer relationships, (6) the global nature of business and health care, and (7) the basic business world challenges, as well. This book provides over 3,200 acronyms and over 850 terms and phrases, representing the biopharma industry language.

Customers of the Biopharma Industry

The complex customer environment and players involved in and with the industry warrant additional introduction. The spectrum of customers and their needs is exceptionally broad for the biopharma industry with at least 11 different categories, each of them both a recipient of communications and a contributor to the biopharma language:

1. Patients with a disease consume the products, along with their families that provide support. Patient support groups are further customers for the biopharma industry.

2. Health care professionals ("providers," i.e., physicians, pharmacists, nurses, and allied healthcare workers) decide upon, guide, and monitor the products' use. They also congregate in national professional associations for communication, education, clinical practice, and research discussions, comprising yet another customer base.

3. The payers in the private and public sectors cover the costs of the products, create reimbursement processes, and provide usage guidelines for products. Private payers include insurance companies, managed care organizations, and the patients. Public payers include federal, state, and local governments.

4. The healthcare systems with the many inpatient and outpatient settings (e.g., hospitals, nursing homes, clinics, physician offices, pharmacies, and laboratories) form a broad and varied context in which patients are treated and the products are used. Usage patterns are impacted by these many settings, and they both facilitate usage and create barriers.

5. The scientific community involves many basic science areas that help discover the products, for example, chemistry, biology, molecular biology, genetics, pharmacology, toxicology, pharmacokinetics, and economics. Each possesses their own terminology that needs to be understood and integrated for product development in the biopharma industry.

6. The clinical research community establishes the benefits and risks for the products in patients through the clinical studies conducted in collaboration with the biopharma industry. Diseases and study designs along with research processes create terminology for biopharma.

7. The many facets of government serve two key functions: performing oversight and regulation of the biopharma industry (the science and the business), and creating the health policies, laws, and regulations governing operations and outcomes (e.g., Food and Drug Administration, Office of Inspector General in the Justice Department, Veterans Administration, National Institute of Health, Health and Human Services, Centers for Medicare and Medicaid Services, Department of Agriculture, and Environmental Protection Agency).

8. Many contractors and vendors in science and business areas support and assist the biopharma industry in performing their work, for example, testing laboratories, contract research organizations, market research companies, sales management organizations, and advertising agencies.

9. The investment community provides the capital to perform the work, monitors the business outcomes and research advances for potential investors, and may even help set corporate goals.

10. The media monitor, report, challenge, and color the work, outcomes, benefits, and risks of the products, product development, and the biopharma business world.

11. The biopharma companies themselves interact through research and business collaborations and alliances and become customers of each other. The biopharma industry engages this breadth of players and customers, leading to substantial complexity, variety, and unique features in its communications, essentially creating a language of its own.

Acronym Usage

The language of biopharma is further complicated by the extensive use of acronyms in the worlds of the sciences, health care, business, and government, in which and with which the biopharma industry must simultaneously operate. Acronyms are used most often to facilitate communications among their user groups, but they may also confuse communication to those staff members and customers unfamiliar with them. A simple acronym (e.g., "EC" or "PC") can have many distinct meanings even within this one industry because of so many different customers, business needs, and technologies. For example, "EC" can mean Executive Committee, or European Commission, or European Council, or Ethics Committee, or enteric coated, or e-clinical, or etoposide with carboplatin. The acronym "PC" can mean placebo control, or physicochemical, or pre-clinical, or product complaints, or primary care, or patient consent, or personal computer, or pediatric committee, or post cibum (Latin for 'after meals'). The context for the acronym is particularly important to guide the reader to the most appropriate definition of the acronym.

Biopharma Industry Department Contributors
The over 4,000 terms, phrases, and acronyms in this book comprise much of the biopharma language and include 10 different work areas of the biopharma industry itself, as noted in Figure 1

Figure 1: Content of Biopharma Language

and in the following comments. Standard business operations (1) and marketing terms (2) are presented regarding all business environments, and are adapted to the science and healthcare context and new product development. Basic research concepts (3) in the acronym and term lists focus on discovery of new molecules and the related processes. Many of the targets and receptors (4) in humans that are recognized as contributing to existing and new molecule discovery are provided. Although any of the thousands of human enzymes, substrates, proteins, metabolites, antibodies, ion channels, ribosomes, DNA/RNA units, and cell receptors could be listed as targets, the about 450 targets/receptors in the book represent current major receptor families and their prominent components. Clinical research terms (5) focus on the many different issues, such as processes, documents, study design issues, clinical assessment tools, people (roles and titles), and activities involved in clinical studies and product development. Clinical assessment tools that could be a scale, index, questionnaire, survey, exam, evaluation, interview, report, schedule, or inventory are incorporated. Government agencies (6) are manifold and varied, and their nomenclatures that impact both the business practices and product development for the biopharma industry are included. Regulatory concepts (7) cited in the book come most often from government health-related agencies that perform oversight of the work (processes and outcomes) of the biopharma industry. The associations and foundations (8) for health care and science professionals that interface with the biopharma industry are noted. Global operations (9) hallmark biopharma product development and marketing, such that many non-U.S. regulatory groups, processes, and other international-related acronyms are addressed as well. Some acronyms for diseases (10) are provided for those likely to appear in case report forms for industry-sponsored studies or in market research for disease and health care information. Drug names are found commonly elsewhere and generally are not included. It is important to note that some of the other science areas are not included, even though they may be used in the biopharma industry, because of their ready availability elsewhere in specialized dictionaries, for example, chemical and trade names for drugs and biological products, anatomic and physiologic names (e.g., muscles, bones, nerves, and blood vessels), and names of microorganisms.

Sources of Acronyms and Terms

The sources to obtain these terms, phrases, and acronyms for the *Handbook of Biopharma Industry Acronyms & Terms* are manifold (described hereafter). Also, they represent the real world environment in which the biopharma industry must operate. The first bases for the handbook are the 30 plus years of hands-on and management experience in healthcare, health education, research, and the industry of the editor and author at two prominent, fully integrated pharmaceutical companies and four start-up companies, as well as six universities, along with his extensive professional contacts through his work with many professional organizations. The book's prestigious editorial board further represents several hundred years, collectively, of healthcare, research, education, and industry experience, supplementing well the content in scope and descriptions.

Industry experience of the editorial board and editor directly involves 14 companies, both pharmaceutical and biotechnological, and both large, fully-integrated and small, start-up companies, that is, Amgen, Amylin, Aventis, Bertek, Boehringer-Ingelheim, Bristol-Myers, Cell-Pro, Cetus, CTI Therapeutics, Hoechst-Marion-Roussel, Marion, Onyx, Pharmacyclics, and Xoma. University affiliations of the editorial board and author have included esteemed research and healthcare institutions such as, Harvard University, Ohio State University, Philadelphia College of Pharmacy and Sciences, University of Buffalo State University, University of California at Los Angeles, University of Florida, University of Kentucky, University of Missouri at Kansas City, University of Southern California, University of Tennessee, and University of Texas. A further industry resource is the annual Drug Information Association meeting every June, which provides a rich, extensive, and diverse source of presentations (hundreds of presentations over four days annually) on every conceivable topic for the industry by industry experts, whether it is a science topic, an operational area, a marketing issue, or a regulatory topic. Journals and periodicals dedicated to drug development and the biopharma industry were used as sources of information for acronyms as well. These include *Nature Reviews Drug Discovery, Nature Biotechnology, Pharmaceutical Executive, Med Ad News, Genetic Engineering News, State of the Clinical Trials Industry, R&D Directions, Center for the Study of Drug Development Impact Re-*

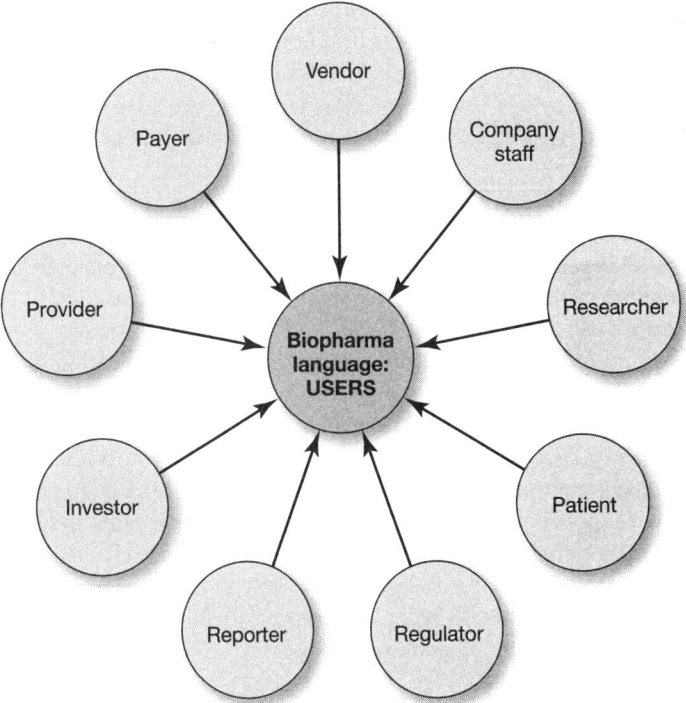

Figure 2: Users of Biopharma Language

ports, FDA Reports to the Nation, the Code of Federal Regulations (312, for drug development), reports of the Pharmaceutical Research and Manufacturers Association and the Biotechnology Industry Organization, and Ernst and Young's annual biotechnology reports.

Users of the Handbook of Biopharma Industry Acronyms & Terms

The likely users of this nomenclature and language book are quite broad, as displayed in Figure 2 and in the following commentary. This book is intended as a resource to and an educational vehicle for the new staff in the biopharma industry in many areas, for example, marketing, sales, or research, as well as their vendors in contract research, marketing, or sales organizations. We hope that their productivity in the industry may be enhanced through better assimilation of the industry language. At universities, the new investigators for clinical trials, as well as the basic scientists in pharmacology, toxicology, pharmaceutics, pharmacokinetics, and molecular biology need to communicate with their industry colleagues.

The healthcare system interfaces with industry in their roles as payers, providers, and administrators with a need to comprehend the language of the biopharma industry. A new government (regulatory or legislative) employee dealing with healthcare and research will need to access a library of terms and acronyms to better understand the industry and improve communication. The media (reporters) and investment company staff need to improve their understanding of the jargon and language of the biopharma industry. Even patients and their families may need such information about terms and acronyms, especially those involved in patient support groups. Overall, a compilation of acronyms and terms supports all these varied groups through more effective communication and collaborations to bring innovative healthcare products to market, in order to improve patient care, reduce patient suffering, and hopefully cure diseases.

DIRECTIONS FOR USING THIS BOOK

Two sections are presented: Acronyms of the Biopharma Language, covering over 3,300 listings, and Terms and Phrases of the Biopharma Language, covering over 850 listings.

1. The acronyms and terms are in alphabetical order based on the first letter or the first word.
2. For the acronyms, each letter of the acronym is defined in the book, and those letters are capitalized in the definitions; for example, "AP" can be Asia-Pacific (market) or Action Potential or Action Plan or Activator Protein (receptor/target) or Angina Pectoris or Adriamycin, Platinol or APproved.
3. It is important to note that an acronym or term can have very different meanings based on its use, such that the user of this book should always consider the context of the item being used in interpreting its definition.
4. The content of the terms and acronyms is the interpretation of the author and editor, along with review by the editorial board.
5. The definitions of any acronym, term, or phrase are presented in practical terms, as much as possible, for more easy understanding by the breadth of the book's readership. They are not official government or organizational definitions.
6. Many acronyms and terms relate to government regulations, and their definitions are paraphrased for readability, but they are as close as possible to publications of the respective government agency.
7. Individual pharmaceutical companies will use an acronym or term and may offer a somewhat different meaning, but the over 4,000 in this book represent commonly used examples to guide the new person working either within or with the biopharma industry.

AUTHOR AND EDITORIAL BOARD

Biography of the Author and Editor:
Ronald P. Evens, PharmD, FCCP

Ronald Evens is CEO and President of M.A.P.S. 4 Biotec, Inc., consulting to biotechnology and pharmaceutical industries for medical affairs and product launches, especially strategy, planning, staffing, and operations for clinical trials (phases 2, 3b, and 4), medical education, publication planning, medical science liaisons, pharmacy affairs, and medical information for marketed and pipeline products (U.S. and International). Dr. Evens is also clinical professor at the University of Florida, College of Pharmacy in the Departments of Pharmaceutics and Pharmacy Practice, teaching about industry and biotechnology. He served on the board of directors for Oragenics, Inc., as well as their interim President and CEO in 2008, Cheladerm (drug company), national advisory boards for University of Florida, Biotechnology Development Incubator, and three Colleges of Pharmacy in the University of Florida, Gainesville; University of Buffalo, Buffalo, New York; and Midwestern University, Chicago, Illinois. Previous boards were HDMA Healthcare Foundation; American Society of Health-Systems Pharmacists, Research and Education Foundation; and industry advisory boards for medical societies in Hematology and Oncology and the American College of Clinical Pharmacy. He has made over 150 presentations on the healthcare industry and published over 100 publications, with 14 book chapters including "Biotechnology" in *Encyclopedia of Pharmaceutical Technology,* 2nd (2002) and 3rd (2006) editions; "Biotechnology Products in the Pipeline" in *Pharmaceutical Biotechnology for Pharmacists and Pharmaceutical Scientists,* 1st (1997) and 2nd (2002) editions. He was also editor of the book, *Drug & Biological Development, From Molecule to Product & Beyond* (2007), published by Springer.

Previously at Amgen for more than 13 years, he created and directed the Professional Services Department, which was responsible for medical information, post-marketing research, and medical communications for marketed products (staff of 140 and budget of $40 million). At Amgen, he also created the PeriApproval Research Group in Clinical Development for late-stage research for pipeline products. Dr. Evens was Associate Director of Clinical Research and Medical Services at Bristol-Myers Squibb for more than 6 years; Associate Professor and later chairman of Department of Pharmacy Practice at the University of Tennessee, Memphis. He created the Drug Information Center and was Assistant and Associate Professor at the University of Texas at Austin and University of Texas Center for Health Sciences. Faculty appointment as clinical professor also occurred at the University of Southern California, College of Pharmacy. His clinical research has been in areas of oncology, nephrology, hepatology, arthritis, infections, pain, and neurology.

Dr. Evens received a Bachelors of Science in Pharmacy at University of Buffalo in New York, and then completed an internship at E.J. Meyer Memorial Hospital in Buffalo. He attended the University of Kentucky for his PharmD and a 3-year residency and later the University of Southern California, Marshall School of Business, where he completed a certificate program for Marketing 101 for Scientists. His academic and professional awards have included Roger Mantsavinos (Biochemistry), Robert Ritz (Pharmacology), Rexall (1st in class), and the Rho Chi Honor Society at University of Buffalo; Resident's "Impact" Award at University of Kentucky; and Fellowship with American College of Clinical Pharmacy.

Editorial Board:

Stephen Carroll, PhD
Position: President, Altair Consulting
Previous Positions: Vice-President, Scientific and Product Development at Xoma LLC; Vice-President of Preclinical Development at Xoma LLC; Director of Protein Chemistry at Xoma LLC; Assistant Professor, Microbiology and Molecular Genetics at Harvard Medical School

Education and Training: PhD in Microbiology from University of California at Los Angeles, Los Angeles, CA; BA in Biology, University of California at San Diego
Resides at Walnut Creek, CA

Joel Covinsky, PharmD, FCCP
Position: Consultant, Research and Development, Pharmaceutical Industry
Previous Positions: Vice-President Global Drug Development, RAPIDe (Global program to optimize product development) at Aventis; Vice-President, Medical Communications and Education at Aventis; Vice-President, Cardiovascular-Renal and Respiratory Medicine at Hoechst Marion Roussel; Vice-President, Cardio-vascular/Gastrointestinal at Marion Merrell Dow; Professor of Medicine and Pharmacy and Director of Clinical Pharmacology and Metabolic Support at University of Missouri College of Medicine and Truman Medical Center
Education and Training: Clinical residency at A.B. Chandler Medical Center at University of Kentucky (3 years) PharmD from University of Kentucky, College of Pharmacy, Lexington, KY; Hospital Pharmacy Resident at University of Pennsylvania; BS in Pharmacy, Philadelphia College of Pharmacy and Sciences, Philadelphia, PA
Honors: Rho Chi Society and Aesculapius Key at Philadelphia College of Pharmacy and Sciences; Founding member, President, and Chairman of Research Institute, American College of Clinical Pharmacy; Fellow of American College of Clinical Pharmacy; Paul F. Parker Award, University of Kentucky; Residency "Impact" award, University of Kentucky
Resides at Lee's Summit, MO

Edward F. Kenney, MS
Position: Biopharmaceutical Consultant to CEO, Onyx Pharmaceuticals
Previous Positions: Executive Vice-President and Chief Business Officer at Onyx Pharmaceuticals; Executive Vice-President and Chief Operating Officer at CTI Therapeutics; Vice-President, Marketing at CellPro; Vice-President, Marketing and Sales, and Strategic Planning and Business Development at Chiron-Cetus;

Product Manager at Boehringer-Ingelheim; Product Manager, Business analyst, and Sales representative at Bristol-Myers; Program Coordinator for Health Professions at Ohio Sate University

Education and Training: Graduate business courses at Syracuse University, Syracuse, NY; M.S. in Natural Resources at Ohio State University, Columbus, OH; BS in Zoology at Ohio State University

Resides in Alamo, CA

ACRONYMS OF THE BIOPHARMA LANGUAGE

A	Asian or Anterior
Å	Angstrom
AA	Administrative Assistant or Amino Acid or Alzheimer's Association or Alcoholics Anonymous or Ara-C, Adriamycin (CA CT AML) or African-American
A1A	Alpha-1 Antitrypsin (receptor/target)
AAA	Automobile Association of America or Alpha-1A-Adrenoreceptor (receptor/target)
AAAAI	American Academy of Allergy, Asthma, and Immunology
AACOP	American Association of Colleges of Osteopathic Medicine
AACP	American Association of Colleges of Pharmacy
AAD	American Academy of Dermatology
AAFP	American Association of Family Physicians
AAGR	Average Accumulated Growth Rate
AAHRPP	Association for the Accreditation of Human Research Protection Programs
AAI	American Association of Immunologists
AAMC	American Association of Medical Colleges
AAN	American Academy of Neurology
AAO	American Academy of Ophthalmology
AAOS	American Academy of Orthopaedic Surgeons
AAP	American Academy of Pediatrics
AAPMR	American Academy of Physical Medicine and Rehabilitation
AAPS	American Association of Pharmaceutical Scientists

A1AR	Alpha-1 Adrenergic Receptor (or -A, or -B) (receptor/target)
A2AR	Alpha-2 Adrenergic Receptor (or -A, -B, or -C) (receptor/target)
AA1R	Alpha-Adenosine-1 (or -1A) Receptor (receptor/target)
AA2R	Alpha-Adenosine-2 (or -2B) Receptor (receptor/target)
AA28R	Adenosine A 28 Receptor (receptor/target)
AARP	American Association of Retired Persons
AASLD	American Association for Study of Liver Diseases
AAT	Alpha-AntiTrypsin (receptor/target)
AAV	Adeno-Associated Virus
AB	AntiBody or AntiBiotic
ABA	Alpha-1B (or -2B)-Adrenoreceptor (receptor/target) or American Bar Association
ABC	ATP-Binding Cassette transporters (receptor/target)
ABE	Acute Bacterial Endocarditis
ABG	Arterial Blood Gases
ABMS	American Board of Medical Specialists
ABO	ABO blood type system
ABP	Arterial Blood Pressure
ABPI	Association of the British Pharmaceutical Industry
ABT	gamma-Amino-n-Butyric Transaminase (receptor/target)
ABVD	Adriamycin, Bleomycin, Vinblastine, Dacarbazine (CA CT HD)
AC	Administrative Coordinator or Alternating Current or Adenylyl Cyclase (receptor/target) or AntiConvulsants or Ante Cibum (Latin for before meals) or Adriamycin, Carmustine (CA CT MM Sarcomas) or Air Conditioning
ACA	Alpha-1C-Adrenoreceptor (receptor/target)
A1C	Glycosylated hemoglobin
ACAT	Acyl-coenzyme A: Cholesterol AcylTransferase (receptor/target)
ACC	American College of Cardiology or Acetyl-CoA Carboxylase (receptor/target)

ACCME	Accreditation Council for Continuing Medical Education
ACCP	American College of Clinical Pharmacy or American College of Chest Physicians or American College of Clinical Pharmacology
ACD	Automatic Call Distribution (telephone hotlines)
ACE	Angiotensin Converting Enzyme (receptor/target) or AcetylCholine Esterase (receptor/target) or Adjusted Current Income
ACEP	American College of Emergency Medicine
ACG	American College of Gastroenterology
ACH	AcetylCHoline (receptor/target) or Adrenal Cortical Hormone
ACIP	Advisory Committee on Immunization Practices (with Centers for Disease Control and Food and Drug Administration)
ACLS	Acute Cardiac Life Support
ACMG	American College of Medical Genetics
ACOG	American College of Obstetricians and Gynecologists
ACOEM	American College of Occupational and Environmental Medicine
ACOPP	Adriamycin, Cyclophosphamide, Oncovin, Procarbazine, Prednisone (CA CT HD)
ACP	American College of Physicians
ACPE	American Council for Pharmaceutical Education
ACPM	American College of Preventive Medicine
ACR	American College of Radiology or American College of Rheumatology or AcetylCholine Receptor (receptor/target) or Adjusted Community Rating (with Center for Medicare and Medicaid Services)
ACR20	American College of Rheumatology 20% improvement score in arthritis (also ACR50, ACR70)
ACS	American Cancer Society or American College of Surgeons or Acute Coronary Syndrome
ACT	Activated Clotting Time
ACTH	AdrenoCorticoTropin Hormone (receptor/target)

AD	ADvertising or ADvertisement or Athletic Director or Alzheimer's Disease or AntiDepressants or Adriamycin, Dacarbazine (CA CT Sarcoma) or Aldehyde Dehydrogenase (receptor/target) or Adenosine Deaminase (receptor/target) or After Death or Area Director (sales or marketing)
ADA	American Diabetes Association
ADAA	Animal Drug Availability Act (1996)
ADC	ADenoCarcinoma
ADCC	Antibody-Dependent Cell-mediated Cytotoxicity
ADCF	Animal Derived Component Free media
ADD	Attention Deficit Disorder
ADEP	AcylDEpsiPeptidolactones (receptor/target)
ADHD	Attention Deficit Hyperactivity Disorder
ADL	Activities of Daily Living
ADME	Adsorption, Distribution, Metabolism, and Excretion
ADMET	Absorption, Distribution, Metabolism, Excretion, and Toxicity
ADO	ADenOsine (receptor/target)
ADR	Adverse Drug Reaction
ADUFA	Animal Drug User Fee Act
AdvaMed	Advanced Medical Technology Association
AE	Adverse Event or Accident and Emergency or ApprovablE (of New Drug Application by Food and Drug Administration)
AEDs	AntiEpileptic Drugs
AERs	Adverse Event Reactions or Adverse Event Reports
AERS	Adverse Event Reporting System (with FDA)
AF	Arthritis Foundation or Atrial Fibrillation or Atrial Flutter
AG	AntiGen or AGent or AGency
AGA	American Gastroenterological Association
AGRP	AGouti-Related Protein (receptor/target)
AGS	American Geriatric Society
AHA	American Hospital Association or American Heart Association

AHC	Academic Health Center
AHCPR	Agency for Health Care Policy and Research
AHEC	Area Health Education Centers
AHFS	American Hospital Formulary Service
AHFS-DI	AHFS-Drug Information (book)
AHRQ	Agency for Healthcare Research and Quality
AIDS	Acquired Immune Deficiency Syndrome
AIMS	Alberta Infant Motor Scale or Arthritis Impact Measurement Scale
AK	AMPA/Kainate (receptor/target)
AKT	Intracellular Kinase signaling enzyme (receptor/target)
AL	ALuminum or ALabama
ALA	American Lung Association or ALAnine
ALG	Arachidonate 5-LipoxyGenase (receptor/target)
ALL	Acute Lymphocytic Leukemia
ALS	Amyotrophic Lateral Sclerosis
ALT	ALanine Transferase
AM	Alternative Medicines (non-FDA regulated products used as therapies) or Morning hours (12:01AM to 11:59 AM)
AMA	American Medical Association or Against Medical Advice
AMC	Academic Medical Center
AMD	Acute Macular Degeneration or Age-related Macular Degeneration
AMCP	Academy of Managed Care Pharmacy
AMDUCA	Animal Medicinal Drug Use Clarification Act (1994)
AMI	Acute Myocardial Infarction
AML	Acute Myeloid Leukemia
AMP	Average Manufacturer's Price or Adenosine MonoPhosphate (receptor/target)
AMPK	AMP-activated protein Kinase (receptor/target)
AMT	Alternative Minimum Tax
AMTI	Alternative Minimum Tax Income
AMWA	American Medical Writer's Association

ANA	American Nurses Association or AntiNuclear Antibodies
ANC	Absolute Neutrophil Count
ANCOVA	ANalysis of COVAriance
ANDA	Abbreviated New Drug Application
ANG	ANGiotensin (receptor/target)
ANLL	Acute NonLymphocytic Leukemia
ANNA	American Nephrology Nursing Association
ANOVA	ANalysis Of VAriance
ANP	Atrial Natriuretic Peptide (receptor/target)
ANR	Agency for National Research (in France)
ANS	Adrenergic Nervous System
ANT	Adenine Nucleotide Translocator 1 (receptor/target)
ANZTPA	Australia and New Zealand Therapeutics Products Authority
AO	Alert and Oriented or Amine Oxidases (receptor/target)
AOA	American Osteopathic Association
AP	Asia-Pacific (market) or Action Potential or Action Plan or Activator Protein (receptor/target) or Angina Pectoris or Adriamycin, Platinol (CA CT OC) or APproved (NDA by FDA)
A&P	Advertising and Promotion
APA	American Psychiatric Association
APAF	Apoptotic Protein Activity Factor-1 (receptor/target)
APC	Ambulatory Payment Classification (government drug pricing) or Antigen Presenting Cell (WBC) or Activated Protein C (receptor/target) or Atrial Premature Contractions
APEC	Asia Pacific Economic Community
APhA	American Pharmaceutical Association
APHA	American Protestant Hospital Association or American Public Health Association
API	Active Pharmaceutical Ingredient or Alpha-1 Proteinase Inhibitor (receptor/target)
APO-2L	APOLipoprotein-2 (receptor/target)

APOB	APO-lipoprotein B (receptor/target)
APRIL	A PRoliferation Inducing Ligand (receptor/target)
APTA	American Physical Therapy Association
APTT	Activated Partial Thromboplastin Time
AQ	AQueous
AQLQ	Asthma Quality of Life Questionnaire
AR	Adenosine Receptor (receptor/target) or Androgen Receptor (receptor/target) or Aldose Reductase (receptor/target)
ARA	American Rheumatism Association or Adenosine Receptor Agonist (receptor/target) or Alpha-Receptor Agonists or Antagonists (receptor/target)
A2RA	Angiotensin 2 Receptor Antagonist
ARB	Adrenergic Receptor Blockade (receptor/target) or Angiotensin Receptor Blocker (receptor/target)
ARC	American Red Cross or American Rheumatism Council
ARD	Acute Respiratory Disease
AREA	Academic Research Enhancement Award (in NIH)
ARF	Acute Renal Failure or ADP Ribosylation Factor (receptor/target)
ARG	ARGinine
ARIS	Adverse Reaction Information System
ARO	Academic Research Organization
AS	Ankylosing Spondylitis or ArterioSclerosis
ASA	American Society of Anesthesiologists or AcetylSalicylic Acid
ASAP	As Soon As Possible
ASC	Amiloride-sensitive Sodium Channel (receptor/target)
ASCI	American Society for Clinical Investigation
ASCN	American Society for Clinical Nutrition
ASCO	American Society of Clinical Oncology
ASCP	American Society of Clinical Pathology or American Society of Consulting Pharmacists
ASCPT	American Society of Clinical Pharmacology and Therapeutics

ASCVD	ArterioSclerotic CardioVascular Disease
ASH	American Society of Hematology
ASHAP	Adriamycin, cisplatin, Ara-C, methylPrednisolone (CA TX NHL)
ASHP	American Society of Health-system Pharmacists
ASIM	American Society of Internal Medicine
ASM	American Society of Microbiology
ASN	American Society of Nephrology or ASparagiNase
ASO	Automatic Stop Order
ASP	ASParaginase or Average Sales Price
ASPS	American Society of Plastic Surgeons
ASQ	American Society for Quality
ASR	Analyte-Specific Reagent
ARS	Adverse ReactionS
ASTRO	American Society for Therapeutic Radiology and Oncology
ASX	ASparaginase or ASpartic acid
AT	AntiThrombin (receptor/target) or AngioTensin (receptor/target) or AminoTransferase (receptor/target) or Approval Time (by FDA for NDA)
ATIII	Anti-Thrombin III (receptor/target)
ATC	Anatomical, Therapeutic, and Chemical (classification system for drugs by WHO)
ATP	Adenosine TriPhosphate
ATRA	All-Trans Retinoic Acid (CA CT AML)
ATS	American Thoracic Society
ATSDR	Agency for Toxic Substances and Disease Registry
AUA	American Urological Association
AUC	Area Under Concentration curve of blood levels (measure of absorption)
AV	AudioVisual or ArterioVenous or Atrial-Ventricular
AVB	Atrial-Ventricular Block
AVDP	Asparaginase, Vincristine, Daunorubicin, Prednisone (CA CT ALL)
AWCS	Adequate and Well-Controlled Study

AWO	Animal Welfare Officer
AWOL	Absent WithOut Leave
AWP	Average Wholesale Price
AZ	AstraZeneca
B	Black or Billion
BA	BioAvailability or Benzyl Alcohol
B1A	Beta-1-Adrenoreceptor (receptor/target)
BAB	Beta-Adrenergic Blocker
BAC	Blood Alcohol Content or Bacterial Artificial Chromosome (receptor/target) or British Accreditation Council or BenzAlkonium Chloride
BACOP	Bleomycin, Adriamycin, Cyclophosphamide, Oncovin, Prednisone (CA TX NHL)
BAD	Biologically Active Drug
BAFR	B-cell Activating Factor Receptor (receptor/target)
BAFO	Best And Final Offer
BAN	British Approved Name
BAR	Beta-Adrenergic Receptor (receptor/target) or Bile Acid Receptor (receptor/target)
BASIS	Behavior And Symptom Identification Scale
BB	BlockBuster (drug) or Beta-Blocker (drugs) or Blood Bank
BBB	Better Business Bureau or Blood Brain Barrier or Bundle Branch Block
BC	Breast Cancer or Before Christ or Birth Control or Blue Cross or BeCause
BCAVE	Bleomycin, Ceenu, Adriamycin, VinblastinE (CA CT HD)
BCBS	Blue Cross and Blue Shield (health insurance)
BCG	Boston Consulting Group or Bacillus Calmette-Guerin vaccine
BCE	ButyrylCholine Esterase (receptor/target)
BCL2	B-Cell Lymphoma-2 protein (receptor/target)
BCP	BCNU, Cyclophosphamide, Prednisone (CA TX MM)
BCPS	Board Certified Pharmaceutical Specialist

BCR	B-Cell Receptor (receptor/target)
BCS	Biopharmaceutics Classification System (with FDA)
BD	Business Development or Birth Defect or BiDimensional or BenzoDiazepine
BDA	BenzoDiazepine Agonist or Antagonist (receptor/target)
BDI	Beck Depression Inventory or Biotechnology Development Incubator
BDNF	Brain Derived Neurotrophic Factor (receptor/target)
BDOPA	Bleomycin, Dacarbazine, Oncovin, Prednisone, Adriamycin (CA TX HD)
BE	BioEquivalence or Biochemical Efficiency or Bacterial Endocarditis
BEP	Bleomycin, Etoposide, Platinol (CA CT Testicular)
BFU	Burst Forming Unit
BHD	BCNU, Hydroxyurea, Dacarbazine (CA TX MM)
BHK	Baby Hamster Kidney (cells)
BHS	Beck Hopelessness Scale
BI	Boehringer Ingelheim Pharmaceuticals, Inc. or Biogen-Idec, Inc.
BIC	Best-In-Class
BID	Bis In Die (Latin for twice a day treatment)
BIMO	BIoresearch MOnitoring initiative (of FDA)
BIO	Biotechnology Industry Organization
BK	BradyKinin (receptor/target)
BLA	Biologics License Application
BLyS	B-Lymphocyte Stimulator (receptor/target)
BM	BioMarkers or Bowel Movement or Boehringer-Mannheim or Bone Marrow or Brain Metastases
BMA	British Medical Association
BMD	Bone Mineral Density
BMI	Body Mass Index
BMJ	British Medical Journal
BMLA	Biological Materials License Agreement (with NIH)
BMP	Bone Morphogenic Protein (receptor/target)
BMQ	Brief Medication Questionnaire

BMR	Basal Metabolic Rate
BMS	Bristol Myers-Squibb
BMT	Bone Marrow Transplant
BMWP	Biological Medicinal products Working Party (in EU)
BN	BillioN
BNP	Brain Natruretic Protein (receptor/target)
BO	Body Odor
BOD	Board Of Directors or Burden Of Disease
BP	Best Practices or Blood Pressure or Binding Proteins or Boiling Point or British Pharmacopoeia
BPA	Blanket Purchase Agreement (with NIH)
BPCA	Best Pharmaceuticals for Children Act (2002)
BPH	Benign Prostatic Hypertrophy
BPI	Brief Pain Inventory
BPM	Breaths Per Minute or Beats Per Minute
BPS	Board of Pharmaceutical Specialties or Brief Psychiatric Scale
BRC	Business Reply Card
BRCA1	Gene defect for repair of DNA tumor suppressor
BRDPI	Biomedical Research and Development Price Index
BRMAC	Biologics Response Modifier Advisory Committee
BRMs	Biologic Response Modifiers
BRT	Botanical Review Team (at FDA)
BS	Blue Shield or Breath Sounds or Bowel Sounds or Bachelors of Science
BSA	Body Surface Area or Bovine Serum Albumin
BSAT	Biological Select Agent and Toxin (receptor/target)
BSI	Behavioral Status Index
BSN	Bachelor of Science in Nursing
BT	BioTechnology or Blood Transfusion or Brain Tumor or Brand Team
BTK	Bruton's Tyrosine Kinase (receptor/target)
BTU	British Thermal Unit
BU	Business Unit
BUD	Beyond Use Dating

BUN	Blood Urea Nitrogen
BW	Body Weight or Black and White
BWI	Bacteriostatic Water for Injection
BWP	Biotechnology Working Group (in Europe)
BZP	BenZodiazePine (receptor/target)
C	Concentration or one hundred (Roman numeral) or Centigrade or Caucasian or Catholic or Control or Constant
C-II	Controlled substance, level 2, requiring a prescription and no refills
C-III	Controlled substance, level 3, requiring a prescription and limited number of refilled prescriptions
C-IV	Controlled substance, level 4, requiring a prescription
C14	Carbon 14 (radioactive material)
CA	CAncer or Corporate Accounts or CAlcium or CAlifornia or Cardiac Arrest or Coronary Artery or Chronological Age or Cytarabine, Asparaginase (CA CT AML and ANLL) or Cancer Antigen or Carbonic Anhydrase (receptor/target)
CABG	Coronary Artery Bypass Graft
CAD	Caspase-Activated DNAse (receptor/target) or Coronary Artery Disease
CAE	Cycophosphamide, Adriamycin, Etoposide (CA CT SCLC)
CAF	Cyclophosphamide, Doxorubicin, Fluorouracil (CA CT Breast)
CAGR	Compound Annual Growth Rate
CAH	Chronic Active Hepatitis or Carbonic AnHydrase (receptor/target)
CAL	CALories
CALC	CALCitonin (receptor/target)
CALGB	Cancer And Leukemia Group B
CAM	Corporate Accounts Manager
CAMP	Cyclic Adenosine MonoPhosphate (receptor/target) or Cyclophosphamide, Adriamycin, Methotrexate, Procarbazine (CA CT NSCLC)

CANDAs	Computer Assisted New Drug Applications
CAP	Competitive Acquisition Program (with CMS) or CAPsule or Community Acquired Pneumonia or Cyclophosphamide, Adriamycin, Platinol (CA CT GU and NSCLC) or Commercialization Assistance Program (in NIH) or Community Assistance Program (in HHS) or CAncer of Prostate
CARES	CAncer Rehabilitation Evaluation System
CAS #	Number for chemical substances from American Chemical Society
CAT	Computerized Axial Tomography (scan) or Computerized Adaptive Testing
CAV	Calcium Anion Voltage channel receptor (receptor/target) or Cyclophosphamide, Adriamycin, Vincristine (CA CT SCLC)
CB	Cost Benefit or CannaBinoid (-1 or -2) (receptor/target) or Code Blue (medical emergency)
CBA	Cost Benefit Analysis
CBC	Complete Blood Count
CBD	CanniBinoiDs (receptor/target)
CBO	Congressional Budget Office
CBER	Center for Biologics Evaluation and Research (in FDA)
CC	Clinical Coordinator or Copy or Cell Culture or Chief Complaint or Carboplatin, Cyclophosphamide (CA CT OV) or Cubic Centimeter or Creatinine Clearance or Chamber of Commerce or ChemoChime
CCA	Comparative Cost Adjustment (in Medicare program)
CCB	Calcium Channel Blockers
CCC	Comprehensive Cancer Center or Cation Chloride Cotransporter (receptor/target)
CCKR	CholeCystoKinin Receptor (receptor/target)
CCN	Comprehensive Cancer Network
CCO	Chief Commercial Officer
CCOP	Community Clinical Oncology Group
CCR	ChemoChime Receptor (1 up to 8) (receptor/target)
CCU	Coronary Care Unit

CD	Complement Determining (region in antibody structure) or Controlled Delivery or CycloDextrins (receptor/target) or Compact Disc or Cytarabine, Daunorubicin (CA CT ANLL) or Crohn's Disease
CDA	Confidential Disclosure Agreement or Commercialization Development Agreement (with NIH) or Calcium-Dependent Antibiotic pathway (receptor/target) or Central Drug Authority (in India)
CDC	Centers for Disease Control (in PHS) or Complement Dependent Cytotoxicity or Carboplatin, Doxorubicin, Cyclophosphamide (CA CT OC)
CDCP	Center for Disease Control and Prevention (in PHS)
CDE	Cyclophosphamide, Doxorubicin, Etoposide (AIDS-lymphoma)
CDER	Center for Drug Evaluations and Research (in FDA)
CDISC	Clinical Data Interchange Standards Consortium
CDK	Cyclin-Dependent Kinase (receptor/target)
CDM	Clinical Data Management or Clinical Data Managers
CDP	Clinical Development Plan
CDR	Complement Determining Region (of Mabs) or Central Document Room (for CDER at FDA)
CDRH	Center for Devices and Radiological Health (in FDA)
Ce	Concentration of a drug for desired Effectiveness
CE	Continuing Education or Cost Effectiveness
CEA	Cost Effectiveness Analysis or Carcinogenic Embryonic Antigen (receptor/target)
CED	Coverage with Evidence Development (CMS requirement for PMC)
CEF	Cyclophosphamide, Epirubicin, Fluorouracil (CA CT Breast)
CEH	Carboxylic Ester Hydrolase (receptor/target)
CEO	Chief Executive Officer
CERA	Continuous Erythropoiesis Receptor Activator (target/receptor)
CERT	Centers for Education and Research on Therapeutics
CETP	Cholesteryl Ester Transfer Protein (receptor/target)
CEU	Continuing Education Unit

CF	Cystic Fibrosis or Cardiac Failure or Cisplatin, Fluorouracil (CA CT HN)
CFA	Consumer Federation of America
CFL	Cisplatin, Fluorouracil, Leucovorin (CA CT HN)
CFM	Cyclophosphamide, Fluorouracil, Mitoxantrone (CA CT Breast)
CFO	Chief Financial Officer
CFPT	Cyclophosphamide, Fluorouracil, Prednisone, Tamoxifen (CA CT Breast)
CFR	Code of Federal Regulations
CFR 312	Code of Federal Regulations (for drug development, IND, and NDA)
CFSAN	Center for Food Safety and Applied Nutrition
CFU	Colony Forming Unit
CG	Clinical Grant or CarcinoGenicity or Cyclo-oxyGenases (receptor/target)
CGD	Chronic Granulomatous Disease
CGMP	Current Good Manufacturing Practices or Cyclic Guanylyl MonoPhosphate (receptor/target)
CGRP	Calcitonin Gene-Related Peptide (receptor/target)
CGT	Ceramide GlucoTransferase (receptor/target)
CH	CHolesterol
CHA	Catholics Hospital Association
CHAD	Cyclophosphamide, Hexamethylmelamine, Adriamycin, DDP (CA CT OC)
CHAP	Cyclophosphamide, Hexamethylmelamine, Adriamycin, Platinol (CA CT OC)
CHD	Coronary Heart Disease
CHF	Congestive Heart Failure
CHG	CHanGe or CHarGe
CHIP	Children's Health Insurance Program (with HHS)
CHK	CHemoKine (receptor/target) or CHeckpoint Kinase (receptor/target)
CHMP	Committee for Medicinal Products for Human Use (in Europe)
CHO	CarboHydrate or Chinese Hamster Ovary (cells)

CHOP	Cyclophosphamide, Hydroxydaunomycin, Oncovin, Prednisone (CA CT NHL) or Children's Hospital Of Philadelphia
CHOP-B	Cyclophosphamide, Hydroxydaunomycin, Oncovin, Prednisone, Bleomycin (CA CT NHL)
CI	Confidence Interval (in statistics, variations around a mean) or Curies (measure of radioactivity) or Continuous Infusion
CIA	Chemotherapy Induced Anemia or Corporate Integrity Agreement (with HHS) or Central Intelligence Agency
CIOMS	Council for International Organizations of Medical Sciences
CIO	Chief Information Officer
CIP	Chromatin ImmunoPrecipitation
CISCA	CISplatin, Cyclophosphamide, Adriamycin (CA CT GU)
CKD	Chronic Kidney Disease
CL	CLearance (of a drug from the body) or Central Laboratories or ChLoride or Confidence Limits
CLCR	CLearance of CReatinine or ChLoride Channel Receptor (receptor/target)
CLD	Chronic Lung Disease
CLIA	Clinical Laboratory Improvement Amendment (with CMS)
CLL	Chronic Lymphocytic Leukemia
CLR	Cysteinyl Leukotriene Receptor (receptor/target)
CLT	Cysteinyl LeukoTrienes (receptor/target)
CMA	Continuous Marketing Application or Cost Minimization Analysis
Cmax	Maximum Concentration (of a drug)
Cmin	Minimum Concentration (of a drug)
CMC	Chemistry, Manufacturing, and Controls (section for NDA)
CMD	Coordination groups for Mutual-recognition and Decentralized procedures (in Europe)
CME	Continuing Medical Education

CMF	Cyclophosphamide, Methotrexate, Fluorouracil (CA CT Breast)
CMFP	Cyclophosphamide, Methotrexate, Fluorouracil, Prednisone (CA CT Breast)
CMFVP	Cyclophosphamide, Methotrexate, Fluorouracil, Vincristine, Prednisone (CA CT Breast)
CML	Chronic Myelogenous Leukemia
CMM	Center for Medicaid Management (in Center for Medicare and Medicaid Services) or Capability Maturity Model (within FDA for Information Technology infrastructure)
CMO	Chief Medical Officer or Contract Manufacturing Organization or Chief Manufacturing Officer
CMR	Comprehensive Medication Review
CMS	Centers for Medicare and Medicaid Services or Contract Marketing Services
CMSO	Center for Medicaid and State Operations (in CMS)
CMTP	Center for Medical Technology Policy
CMV	CytoMegaloVirus or Cisplatin, Methotrexate, Vinblastine (CA CT GU)
CNC	Controlled Non-Classified room (in manufacturing)
CNDA	Computer assisted New Drug Application
CNI	CalciNeurin Inhibitor (receptor/target)
CNO	Chief Nursing Officer
CNS	Central Nervous System
CNT	Concentrative Nucleoside Transporter (receptor/target)
CNTF	Ciliary NeuroTrophic Factor (receptor/target)
CO	Commercial Operations or Commanding Officer or Carbon MonOxide or COrporate or COmpany
CO2	Carbon dioxide
COAP	Cyclophosphamide, Oncovin, Ara-C, Prednisone (CA CT Leukemias)
COB	Chairman Of the Board or Cisplatin, Oncovin, Bleomycin (CA CT HN)
COBIT	Control OBjective for Information and related Technology

COBRA	Consolidated Omnibus Budget Reconciliation Act (1985)
COC	Chamber Of Commerce
COD	Committee on Drugs (in FDA or many medical societies) or Cash-On-Delivery or Carbon diOxide Demand (industry requirement in Europe)
COE	Center Of Excellence
COG	Cyclo-OxyGenase (receptor/target) or Children's Oncology Group
COGS	Cost Of Goods Sold
COI	CO-Investigator or Centers Of Influence or Cost Of Illness or Conflict-Of-Interest
COL	Cut-Off Level
COLD	Chronic Obstructive Lung Disease
COM	Composition Of Matter (in patents)
COMIS	Centerwide Oracle-based Management Information System (in FDA for Adverse Event tracking in phase 4 studies)
COMLA	Cyclophosphamide, Oncovin, Methotrexate, Leucovorin, Ara-C (CA CT NHL)
COMP	Committee on Orphan Medicinal Products (in Europe) or Cyclophosphamide, Oncovin, Methotrexate, Prednisone (CA CT Lymphoma)
COMT	Catechol-O-Methyl Transferase (receptor/target)
COO	Chief Operating Officer
COP	Clinical Operations Plan or Cyclophosphamide, Oncovin, Prednisone (CA CT NHL)
COPD	Chronic Obstructive Pulmonary Disease
COPE	Commitment, Opportunity, Promise, and Evidence (4 criteria for marketing at product launch) or Cyclophosphamide, Oncovin, Platinol, Etoposide (CA CT Brain)
COPP	Cyclophosphamide, Oncovin, Procarbazine, Prednisone (CA CT NHL)
COS	Certificate of Suitability (of monographs of the European Pharmacopoeia)
COX	CycloOXigenase enzyme -1, -2 (receptor/target)

Cp	Concentration in Plasma (of a drug or chemical)
CP	Cyclophosphamide, Platinol (CA CT OC) or Chest Pain or Clinical Pharmacology or Carrier Protein or Communication Plan
CPA	Certified Public Accountant or Cardio-Pulmonary Arrest or CarboxyPeptidase A (receptor/target) or CycloPhilin A (receptor/target)
CPB	CycloPhilin B (receptor/target)
CPE	Chemical Penetration Enhancers or Complete Physical Exam
CPG	Compliance Program Guidance (with OIG for gifts and marketing)
CPI	Consumer Price Index or Critical Path Initiative (in FDA)
CPK	Creatine PhosphoKinase (receptor/target)
CPM	Capacity Planning and Management or Counts Per Minute
CPMP	Committee for Proprietary Medicinal Products (in Europe)
CPO	Chief Pharmacy Officer
CPOE	Computerized Physician Order Entry
CPR	Cardio-Pulmonary Resuscitation
CPSC	Consumer Products Safety Commission
CPSN	Community Pharmacy Safety Network
CPT	(Journal of) Clinical Pharmacology and Therapeutics
CPT Code	Common Procedure Terminology codes
CQI	Continuous Quality Improvement
CR	Complete Response or Clinical Research or CReatinine
CRA	Clinical Research Associate
CRADA	Cooperative Research And Development Agreement (with NIH)
CRC	Clinical Research Center or Clinical Research Coordinator or ColoRectal Cancer
CRCL	CReatinine CLearance
CRF	Corticotrophin Releasing Factor (receptor/target) or Chronic Renal Failure

CRHR	Corticotrophin Releasing Hormone Receptor (receptor/target)
CRIM	Cross Reactive Immunologic Material
CRISP	Computer Retrieval of Information on Scientific Programs (In NIH)
CRIX	Clinical Regulatory Information eXchange
CRM	Customer Relationship Management or Clinical Research Manager or Continual Reassessment Method (in dose determinations)
CRO	Clinical Research Organization or Contract Research Organization
CRT	Controlled Randomized Trial or Case Report Tabulations (in FDA filings)
CS	Clinical Safety or Customer Services or CorticoSteroids
CSA	Controlled Substances Act or Consulting Services Agreement
CSD	Cambridge Structural Database
CSDD	Center for the Study of Drug Development (at Tufts University)
CSF	Critical Success Factors or Colony Stimulating Factor or Cerebral Spinal Fluid
CSL	Clinical Science Liaison
CSM	Clinical Supplies Management or Committee on Safety of Medicines (in the United Kingdom)
CSO	Contract Service Organization or Contract Sales Organization or Consumer Safety Officer (in FDA) or Chief Scientific Officer
CSR	Clinical Study Review (groups at NIH) or Clinical Study Report or Case Safety Report or Center of Scientific Review (in NIH)
Css	Concentration at Steady State
CSS	Clinical Support Specialist or Contract Sales Services
CST	Central Standard Time (United States)
CT	Cell Therapy or Clinical Trial or ChemoTherapy or Clotting Time or Computed Tomography or

Cytarabine, Thioguanine (CA CT AML) or Cisplatin, Taxol (CA CT OV) or Coated Tablet

CTA Clinical Trials Application (European IND equivalent) or Center for Technology Assessment (International organization) or Clinical Trials Agreement

CTC Common Toxicity Criteria (from National Cancer Institute)

CTD Common Technical Document (for all information for FDA and EMEA Submissions leading to product approval)

CTEP Cancer Treatment Evaluation Program (in NCI)

CTI Council for Technology and Innovation (in CMS and FDA)

CTL Cytotoxic T-Lymphocyte (receptor/target)

CTLA Cytotoxic T-Lymphocyte associated Antigen (receptor/target)

CTM Clinical Trials Materials or Clinical Trials Management or Community TradeMark (European Trademark)

CTMB Clinical Trials Monitoring Branch (in NCI)

CTMS Clinical Trial Management System

CTO Chief Technical Officer

CTR Clinical Trials Registry

CU Cost Utility or CUries

CUA Cost Utility Analysis

CV CardioVascular or Curriculum Vitae or Coefficient of Variation or CerebroVascular or Cisplatin, Vepesid (CA CT–SCLC, NSCLC) or Comparison Value (chemicals) or Cell Volume or Cancer Vaccine

CVA CerebroVascular Accident

CVD CardioVascular Disease or Cisplatin, Vinblastine, Dacarbazine (CA CT Melanoma)

CVEB Cisplatin, Vinblastine, Etoposide, Bleomycin (CA CT GU)

CVI Carboplatin, Vepesid, Iphosphamide (CA CT NSCLC)

CVM	Center for Veterinary Medicine (in FDA) or CardioVascular Medicine
CVMP	Committee for Veterinary Medicinal Products (in Europe)
CVP	Central Venous Pressure or Cyclophosphamide, Vincristine, Prednisone (CA CT Leukemias, NHL)
CVPP	CeeNU, Vinblastine, Procarbazine, Prednisone (CA CT Lymphoma)
CVS	CardioVascular System or CVS (retail pharmacy company)
CY	Calendar Year
CYA	CYclophosphamide, Adriamycin (CA CT Neuroblastoma)
CYADIC	CYclophosphamide, Adriamycin, Dacarbazine (CA CT Sarcomas)
CYP	CYtochrome P450 (isoenzymes in liver metabolism of drugs)
CYS	CYSteine
CYT	CYTokine
CYVADIC	CYclophosphamide, Vincristine, Adriamycin, Dacarbazine (CA CT Sarcomas)
CX	Cure
CXCR	Chemokine Receptor (receptor/target)
D	Dose or Day or Dextrose or Divorced or Dead or Dalton
D1	Dopamine-1 (or -2, -3, -4, or -5) (receptor/target)
DA	Drug Availability or DopAmine (-1, -2, -3, or -4) (receptor/target) or District Attorney or DAlton or Daunorubicin, Ara-C (CA CT AML and ANLL) or Dosage and Administration or Decision Analysis
D&A	Dosage and Administration
DAC	Drug Advisory Committee (in FDA, 14 committees based on drug therapeutic groups) or Data Audit Committee
DAG	DiAcylGlycerol (receptor/target)

DAI	Drug Attitude Inventory
DALE	Disability Adjusted Life Expectancy
DARPA	Defense Advanced Research Projects Agency
DAR	DopAmine Receptor family (-2, -3, -4) (receptor/target)
DAS	Disease Activity Score
DAT	Daunorubicin, Ara-C, Thioguanine (CA CT AML) or DopAmine Transporter (receptor/target) or Drug Abuse Testing
DAV	Daunorubicin, Ara-C, Vepesid (CA CT AML) or Disabeled American Veteran
DAWN	Drug Abuse Warning Network
DB	Double-Blind or DataBase or Date of Birth
DBP	Diastolic Blood Pressure
DBPCRT	Double-Blind Placebo Controlled Randomized Trial
DC	Dendritic Cells or Direct Current or DisContinue or Drug Consults or Daunorubicin, Cytarabine (CA CT ANLL) or District of Columbia
D&C	Dilatation and Curettage
DCF	Discounted Cash Flow
DCGI	Drugs Controller General of India
DCJI	Disposable Cartridge Jet Injector
DCM	Data Collection and Management
DCP	DeCentralized Procedure (in EU for MRP)
DCPM	Daunorubicin, Cytarabine, Prednisone, Mercaptopurine (CA CT AML)
DCT	Daunorubicin, Cytarabine, Thioguanine (CA CT ANLL)
DD	Differential Diagnosis
DDD	Defined Daily Dose (in WHO classification system for drugs)
DDI	Drug–Drug Interactions
DDMAC	Division of Drug Marketing, Advertising, and Communications (in FDA)
DDP-4	DiPeptidyl Peptidase-4 (receptor/target)
DDS	Doctor of Dental Sciences or Doctor of Dental Surgery

DDR1	Discoidin Domain Receptor 1
DEA	Drug Enforcement Agency
DERP	Drug Effectiveness Review Program (at Oregon HSC for state medicaids)
DES	Dissociative Experiences Scale or DieEthylStilbestrol
DFS	Disease Free Survival
DGAT-1	Fat inhibitor enzyme system (receptor/target)
DH	Department Head
DHAP	Dexamethasone, Ara-C, Platinol (CA CT NHL)
DHFR	DiHydroFolate Reductase (receptor/target)
DHHS	Department of Health and Human Services
DHOR	DiHyroOrotate Reductase (receptor/target)
DHS	Department of Homeland Security
DI	Drug Information or Drug Interaction or Disability Index or Doxorubicin, Iphosphamide (CA CT Sarcoma) or Diabetes Insipidus
DIA	Drug Information Association
DIC	Drug Information Center or Disseminated Intravascular Coagulopathy
DIJ	Drug Information Journal
DIR	Division of Intramural Research (in NIH) or DIRector
Div	Dose by intravenous route or Division
DJIA	Dow Jones Industrial Average
DKA	Diabetic KetoAcidosis
DLE	Drug Literature Evaluation or Disseminated Lupus Erythematosus
D5LR	Dextrose 5% in Lactated Ringers
DLT	Dose Limiting Toxicity
DM	District Manager (in sales) or Data Management or Document Management or Diabetes Mellitus or DextroMethorphan
DMARD	Disease Modifying Anti-Rheumatic Drug
DMC	Data Monitoring Committee or Dactinomycin, Methotrexate, Cyclophosphamide (CA CT Trophoblastic)
DME	Durable Medical Equipment

DMF	Drug Master File
DMO	Disease Management Organization
DMP	Data Management Plan
DMSC	Data Management and Safety Committee
DMSO	DiMethylSulfOxide (receptor/target)
DNA	DeoxyriboNucleic Acid or Does Not Apply
DNAP	DNA Polymerase (receptor/target)
DNDI	Drugs for Neglected Diseases Initiative
DNMT1	DNa MethylTransferase-1 (receptor/target)
DNR	Do Not Resuscitate or Did Not Respond
D5NS	Dextrose 5% in Normal Saline
DO	Doctor of Osteopathy or Diet Order or Directors and Officers
D&O	Directors and Officers
DOA	Department Of Agriculture or Dead On Arrival or Delegation Of Authority or Date Of Admission
DOB	Date Of Birth
DOC	Department Of Commerce or Drug Of Choice or DOCument
DOD	Department Of the Defense or Date Of Death or DihydroOrotate Dehydrogenase (receptor/target)
DODP	Division of Oncology Drug Products (in FDA)
DOE	Department Of Energy or Design Of Experiment or Dyspnea On Exertion
DOG	DiOxyGenase (receptor/target)
DOH	Department Of Health
DOJ	Department Of Justice
DOL	Department Of Labor or Division Of Labor
DON	Director Of Nursing
DOP	Director Of Pharmacy
DOR	Delta Opioid Receptor (receptor/target)
DOT	Department Of Treasury
DOTCDP	Division of Over-The-Counter Drug Products (in FDA)
DP	Drug Product
DPD	DihydroPyrimidine Dehydrogenase (receptor/target)

DPM	Doctor of Podiatric Medicine
Dpo	Dose by per os (Latin for oral route)
DPPIV	DiPeptidyl Peptidase IV (receptor/target)
DPS	DihydroPteroate Synthase (receptor/target)
DPT	Diphtheria-Pertussis-Tetanus vaccine
DR	Discipline Review (letter from FDA) or DoctoR or Delivery Room or Drug Related or Dopamine Receptor (receptor/target)
DRA	Deficit Reduction Act (2005)
DRG	Diagnosis Related Group (numbering system for diseases used in billing for healthcare services)
DRL	Discipline Review Letter (from FDA)
DRO	Dihydroorotate Oxidase (receptor/target)
DRR	Drug Regimen Review
DS	Double Strength or Discharge Summary
DSB	Double Stranded Breaks
DSC	Differential Scanning Calorimetry
DSI	Division of Scientific Investigation (in FDA)
DSM	Disease State Management or Diagnostic and Statistical Manual (of Mental Disorders)
DSMB	Data Safety Monitoring Board
DSMC	Data Safety and Monitoring Committee
DSOB	Drug Safety Oversight Board (in FDA)
DST	Daylight Saving Time
DT	Delirium Tremens or Diphtheria Toxin or Diet Therapy
DTC	Direct-To-Consumer (advertising)
DTI	Direct Thrombin Inhibitor
DTIC-ACTD	Dacarbazine, Dactinomycin (CA CT MM)
DTP	Direct-To-Patient (advertising) or Developmental Therapeutics Program (in NCI)
dsRNA	double-stranded RiboNucleic Acid (receptor/target)
DUE	Drug Use Evaluation
DUI	Driving Under the Influence
DUR	Drug Utilization Review

DVM	Doctor of Veterinary Medicine
DVP	Daunorubicin, Vincristine, Prednisone (CA CT ALL)
DVT	Deep Vein Thrombosis
DW	Distilled Water or Dextrose in Water
D5W	Dextrose 5% in Water
DX	Diagnosis
DZ	DiaZepam or Disease

E	Euro (currency in European Union) or Electrode or Estrone or Estimate or East or Energy
Es (6+6)	Essentials of leadership
EA	Environmental Analysis or EAch
EAA	Essential Amino Acids
EAC	Estimated Acquisition Cost
EACA	Epsilon-AminoCaproic Acid (receptor/target)
EAP	Expanded Access Program or Etoposide, Adriamycin, Platinol (CA CT Gastric)
E-AR	Ephrin type-A Receptor (receptor/target)
EBC	Exhaled Breath Concentrate
EBI	European Bioinformatics Institute
EBIDTA	Earnings Before Interest, Depreciation, Taxes, and Amortization
EBM	Evidence-Based Medicine
EMS	EMbryonic Stem cell or Emergency Medical System
EC	European Community or European Council or Enteric Coated or E-Clinical or Executive Committee or European Commission or Ethics Committee or Etoposide, Carboplatin (CA CT SCLC or NSCLC)
ECF	Epirubicin, Cisplatin, Fluorouracil (CA CT Gastric) or Extended Care Facility
ECG	ElectroCardioGram
ECHO	Efficacy, Cost, Humanistic, and Outcome model (for evaluations of drug's impact on healthcare as well as patients)
ECJ	European Court of Justice

ECOG	Eastern Cooperative Oncology Group
ECT	ElectroConvulsive Therapy
eCTD	electronic Common Technical Document
ED	Emergency Department (of a hospital) or Erectile Dysfunction or EpiDural or Erythemal Dose or Educational Development
ED50	Effective Dose in 50% of animals or subjects
EDC	Electronic Data Capture
EDI	Electronic Data Interchange (with FDA for AE reports)
EDMS	Electronic Data Management System
EDQM	European Directorate for the Quality of Medicines
EDS	Electronic Data Systems
DSS	expanded Disability Status Scale
EDTA	EthylDiamineTetraAcetic Acid
EEG	ElectroEncephaloGram
EENT	Eyes, Ears, Nose, and Throat
EEO	Equal Employment Opportunity
EFA	Essential Fatty Acids
EFPIA	European Federation of Pharmaceutical Industries and Associations
EGAPP	Evaluation of Genomic Applications in Practice and Prevention (in CDC)
EGFR	Epidermal Growth Factor Receptor (receptor/target)
EGO	Edging God Out
EH	Epoxide Hydrolase (receptor/target)
EHR	Electronic Health Record
eIND	electronic Investigational New Drug application
EIN	Employer Identification Number (for Internal Revenue Service in U.S.)
EIR	Establishment Inspection Report (for FDA inspections of manufacturing)
EKG	ElectrocardioGram
ELA	Establishment License Application (by FDA for biological manufacturing)
ELF	Etoposide, Leucovorin, Flourouracil (CA CT Gastric)

ELIPS	Electronic Labeling Information Processing System (at FDA using XML system)
ELISA	Enzyme Linked ImmunoSorbent Assay
EM	Electron Microscopy or Extensive Metabolizer
E&M	Evaluation and Management (CPT codes for Medicare billing)
EMA	Etoposide, Mitoxantrone, Ara-C (CA CT ANLL)
Emax	Effective MAXimum (concentration of a drug)
EMEA	European Medicines Evaluation Agency (also known as European Agency for Evaluation of Medicinal Products)
EMS	Emergency Medical Service
EMT	Endocannabinoid Membrane Transporter (receptor/target) or Emergency Medical Technician or Epithelial to Mesenchymal Transition
EN	Enteral Nutrition
ENaC	Epithelial sodium Channel (receptor/target)
ENOS	Endothelial Nitric Oxide Synthase (receptor/target)
ENT	Ear, Nose, and Throat or Equilibrative Nucleoside Transporter (receptor/target)
EOC	Epithelial Ovarian Cancer
EOP1	End Of Phase 1 (meeting with FDA)
EOP2	End Of Phase 2 (meeting with FDA)
EORTC	European Oncology Research and Treatment Consortium
EP	European Parliament or Etoposide, Platinol (CA CT adenocarcinoma and NSCLC) or End-Points or EnkePhalins (receptor/target) or European Pharmacopoeia
E&P	Earnings and Profits
EPA	Environmental Protection Agency
EPC	European Patent Convention or Evidence-based Practice Centers (CMS program for PMC research consortias)
EPI	EPInephrine
EPO	European Patent Office or ErythroPOietin

EPR	Enhanced Permeability and Retention effect or ErythroPoietin Receptor (receptor/target)
EPS	Earnings Per Share or Extra-Pyramidal Symptoms or Exercise Performance Status
EPT	Early Pregnancy Test
EQ	EQuivalent or EQual
ER	Emergency Room or Extended Release or Estrogen Receptor (receptor/target) or Enoyl Reductase (receptor/target)
ERCC	Excision Repair Cross Complementation group 1 gene (receptor/target) or External RNA Control Consortium
ERK	Extracellular signal-Regulated Kinase (receptor/target)
ERN	Employer Resource Network
ERP	Enterprise Resource Planning or Excision Repair Protein-1 (receptor/target)
ERS	Electronic Regulatory Submission or Extended Release Schedule
ERT	Estrogen Replacement Therapy or Enzyme Replacement Therapy
ES	Extra Strength or Embryonic Stem cells
ESA	Erythropoiesis Stimulating Activator (receptor/target)
ESBL	Extended Spectrum Beta-Lactamase bacteria
ESC	Embryonic Stem Cells
eSDI	electronic Source Data Interchange
ESG	Electronic Submissions Gateway (FDA initiative)
ESHAP	Etoposide, Ara-C, methylPrednisolone, Platinol (CA TX NHL)
ESP	Extra Sensory Perception
ESR	Erythrocyte Sedimentation Rate
ESRD	End Stage Renal Disease (program of Medicare for kidney failure)
EST	Expressed Sequence Tags or ESTimate or Eukaryotic Sterol Transporter family (receptor/target) or Eastern Standard Time (United States)
ET	EndoThelin (1) (receptor/target) or EndoToxin
ETF	Exchange Traded Funds

ETT	Exercise Tolerance Test
EU	European Union or Endotoxin Units
EUCAST	European Union Committee on Antimicrobial Susceptibility Testing
EudraCT	European database for Clinical Trials
EULA	End User License Agreement
EUR	EURos or EURope
EV	Enterprise Value or EudraVigilance
EVA	Etoposide, Vinblastine, Adriamycin (CA CT Hodgkin's)
EVMDP	EudraVigilance Medicinal Products Dictionary
EVP	Executive Vice-President
E&Y	Ernst and Young, LLC (consulting group)
EWOC	Escalation (in dosing) With Overdose Control
EWP	Expert Working Party (in Europe)
EX	EXercise or EXamination or EXcluding or EXample or prior relationship
EXPIND	EXPloratory IND
F	Female or Fraction or Fahrenheit (temperature) or Fluorine or Frequency or Father
F2	blood Factor 2 (fibrinogen to fibrin in coagulation cascade)
F7	blood Factor 7 (in coagulation cascade)
F8	blood Factor 8 (in coagulation cascade)
F9	blood Factor 9 (in coagulation cascade)
F10	blood Factor 10 (in coagulation cascade)
FA	Fatty Acid or Folic Acid or FAther
FAAH	Fatty Acid Amide Hydrolase (receptor/target)
Fab	Fragment of an AntiBody (at variable light chain region)
FAC	Fluorouracil, Adriamycin, Cyclophosphamide (CA CT Breast)
FACA	Federal Advisory Committee Act (1972)
FACP	Fellow of American College of Pharmacology
FACS	Fluorescence Activated Cell Sorter assay

FACT	Functional Assessment of Cancer Therapy
FAK	Focal Adhesion Kinase (receptor/target)
FAM	Fluorouracil, Adriamycin, Mitomycin C (CA CT GI and NSCLC)
FAMTX	Fluorouracil, Adriamycin, MeThotreXate (CA CT Gastric)
FAME	Fluorouracil, Adriamycin, Mitomycin C (CA CT GI)
FAP	Fluorouracil, Adriamycin, Platinol (CA CT Gastric)
FAQ	Frequently Asked Question
FAR	Federal Acquisition Regulations
FASB	Financial Accounting Standards Board
FAX	Facsimile (copy sent over the telephone line)
FBS	Fasting Blood Sugar
Fc	Fragment of Constant region of an antibody
FC	Functional Capacity
FCC	Federal Commerce Commission
FCCC	Fox Chase Cancer Center
FCCP	Fellow of the American College of Clinical Pharmacy
FCE	Fluorouracil, Cisplatin, Etoposide (CA CT GI)
FCF	Free Cash Flow
FCL	Fluorouracil, Calcium, Leucovorin (CA CT Colon)
FCR	Fludarabine, Cyclophosphamide, Rituxan (CA TX CLL)
FDA	Food and Drug Administration
FDAMA	Food and Drug Administration Modernization Act (1997)
FDC	Fixed Dose Combinations
FDC Act	Food, Drug, and Cosmetics Act (1907)
FDI	Functional Disability Index
FDLI	Food Drug Law Institute
FD&C	Food, Drug, and Cosmetic Act
FDP	Federal Demonstration Project
FDPS	Farnesyl DiPhosphate Synthase (receptor/target)
FED EX	FEDeral EXpress (for rapid delivery of packages)
FEHBP	Federal Employees Health Benefits Program
FEMA	Flavor and Extract Manufacturers Association or Federal Emergency Management Agency

FEV1	Forced Expiratory Volume in 1 second
FFA	Free Fatty Acids
FFP	Federal Financial Participation
FFS	Fee For Service
FGFR	Fibroblast Growth Factor Receptor (receptor/target)
FHX	Family History
F-I-C	First In Class
FICA	Federal Insurance Corporation of America
FIFO	First In, First Out (method to assess inventory costs)
FIGO	Federation Internationale Gynecologic Organization staging system
FIM	First In Man (PK phase 1 studies)
FIP	Federation Internationale Pharmaceutica
FIPCO	Fully Integrated Pharmaceutical COmpany
FISH	Fluorescent Immunohistochemical in Situ Hybridization
FK BP	FK506 Binding Protein 1a (receptor/target)
FL	FLuid or Flutamide, Leuprolide (CA CT GU)
FLe	Fluorouracil, LEvamisole (CA CT Colon)
FLIC	Functional Living Index in Cancer
FM	Family Medicine
FMEA	Failure Mode and Effects Analysis
FMH	Family Medical History
FMLPR	n-Formyl-Methionyl-Leucyl-Phenylalanine Receptor (receptor/target)
FMN	Flavin MonoNucleotide (receptor/target)
FMS	Fluorouracil, Mitomycin C, Streptozocin (CA CT Pancreas)
FMV	Fair Market Value or Fluorouracil, Methyl-CCNU, Vincristine (CA CT Colon)
FN	Febrile Neutropenia
FOB	Free On Board (inventory of product at company) or Follow-On Board or Foot Of Bed or Follow-On Biologic
FOI	Freedom of Information
FOIA	Freedom Of Information Act

FOMi	Fluorouracil, Oncovin, MItomycin C (CA CT NSCLC)
FOP	Follow-On Product
FP	Family Practice or Framework Programs (in EU, funding R&D) or Freezing Point or Family Planning
FP7	Framework Programme 7 (EC program to stimulate drug innovation in Europe)
FPFV	First Patient First Visit
FPI	Full Prescribing Information
FPL	Federal Poverty Level or Final Printed Labeling
FPQ	Family Pain Questionnaire
FR	Federal Register or Final Report or FRance
FRC	Forced Residual Capacity
FRCP	Fellow of Royal College of Physicians
FSH	Follicle Stimulating Hormone
FSQ	Functional Status Questionnaire
FSR	Federal Status Report
FSS	Federal Supply Schedule
FT	Fast Track (designation by FDA for a product) or FooT or Free Time
FTA	Free Trade Agreement
FTC	Federal Trade Commission
FTE	Full Time Equivalent (one staff person)
FTI	Farnesyl Transferase Inhibitor (receptor/target)
FTT	Failure To Thrive
FU	Follow-Up or FluoroUracil
FUL	Federal Upper Limits (of payments)
FUO	Fever of Unknown Origin
Fx	Fracture or Function
FY	Fiscal Year
FYEO	For Your Eyes Only
FYI	For Your Information
FZ	Flutamide, Zoladex (CA CT GU)
G	Gram or Glucose
G1	Globulin-1

GA	General Anesthesia
G&A	General and Administrative (costs)
GAB	Grb2-Associated Binding protein (receptor/target)
GABA	GabaAminoButyric Acid (receptor/target)
GABAT	Gamma-AminoButyric Acid Transporter (receptor/target) or Gamma-AminoButyric Acid Transaminase (receptor/target)
GAF	Global Assessment of Function scale
GAO	General Accounting Office (of U.S. Congress)
GAP	Gtpase Activating Protein (receptor/target) or Good Animal Practices
GAS	Global Assessment Scale
GATT	General Agreement on Tariffs and Trade (1994)
GAVI	Global Alliance for Vaccines and Immunization
GBM	GlioBlastoma Multiforme
GBT	Global Brand Team
GC	Gas Chromatography (in drug analysis) or GonoCocci or Guanylyl Cyclase (receptor/target)
GCD	Global Clinical Director
GCG	GluCaGon (receptor/target)
GCL	Global Clinical Leader
GCP	Good Clinical Practices or Global Clinical Plan
GCR	GlucoCorticoid Receptor (receptor/target)
GCS	GlucosylCeramide Synthase (receptor/target)
GDNF	Glial-Derived Neurotrophic Factor (receptor/target)
GDP	Gross Domestic Product or Good Document Practices
GDR	Generic (drug) Dispensing Rate
GDS	Geriatric Depression Scale or Genomic Data Submission (to FDA)
GE	GastroEnterology or General Electric company
GEF	Guanine-nucleotide Exchange Factor (receptor/target)
GEMM	Genetically Engineered Mouse Model
GEN	GENetics or GENeral
GEO	Gene Expression Omnibus database

Gentox	GENetic TOXicity
GERD	GastroEsophageal Reflux Disease
GF	Growth Factor
GFP	Green Flourescent Protein (receptor/target)
GFR	Glomerular Filtration Rate
GG	Glyceryl Guaiacolate
GGTP	Gamma GlutarylTransPeptidase (receptor/target)
GHQ	General Health Questionnaire
GHR	Growth Hormone Receptor (receptor/target)
GHRH	Growth Hormone Releasing Hormone (receptor/target)
GHRI	General Health Rating Index
GI	GastroIntestinal
GILI	GastroIntestinal Lipase Inhibitor (receptor/target)
GIP	Gastric Intestinal Polypeptide (receptor/target) or Glucose-dependent Insulinotropic Peptide (receptor/target)
GIS	Geographic Information System
GIT1	G-protein-coupled receptor kinase InTeractor 1 (receptor/target)
GL	Gastric Lipase (receptor/target)
GLN	GLutamiNe
GLP	Good Laboratory Practice or Glucagon-Like Peptide (receptor/target)
GLU	GLUtamate (receptor/target)
GLY	GLYcine
GLX	GLutamine or GLutamic acid
GM	Genetically Modified or General Manager or GraM or Gross Margin
GMO	Genetically Modified Organism or Grants Management Office (in NIH)
GMP	Good Manufacturing Practices or Guanosine MonoPhosphate (receptor/target)
GNP	Gross National Product
GNRH	GoNadotropin Releasing Hormone (receptor/target)
GOG	Gynecologic Oncology Group

GOT	Glutamic Oxaloacetic Transaminase
GP	General Practitioner or GlycoProtein or GlycoPeptides or Generic Product
GP IIb/IIIa	GlycoProteins for platelet aggregation (receptor/target)
GPA	Generic drug Pharmaceutical Association
GPCR	G-Protein Coupled Receptor (receptor/target)
GPhA	Generic drug Pharmaceutical Association
GPL	Global Project Leader or Global Product Leader
GPO	Group Purchase Organization or Government Printing Office
G6PD	Glucose-6-Phospate Dehydrogenase (receptor/target)
GPR	Glucagon-like Peptide-1 Receptor (receptor/target) or GlycoProtein Receptor (receptor/target)
GPT	Glutamic Pyruvic Transaminase (receptor/target) or Global Project Team or Global Product Team
GPvP	Good PharmacoVigilance Practices
GR	Glutamate Receptor (receptor/target) or Glucocorticoid Receptor (receptor/target) or GRain or Glucagon Receptor (receptor/target)
GRAS	Generally Regarded As Safe
GRFT	Glycinamide Ribonucleotide Formyl Transferase (receptor/target)
GRK	G-coupled Receptor Kinase (receptor/target)
GRMP	Good Review Management Practices
GRP	Good Regulatory Practices or Good Review Practices
GS	GlycoSidases (receptor/target) or Grade Scale
GSK	GlaxoSmithKline, Inc. or Glycogen Synthetase Kinase (receptor/target)
GSP	Good Sales Practices
GST	Glutathione S-Transferase (receptor/target)
GT	Glucose Tolerance or GlycosylTransferase (receptor/target) or GenoToxicity or Gene Therapy
GTT	Glucose Tolerance Test
GTP	Good Tissue Practices
GU	GenitoUrinary

GVHD	Graft Versus Host Disease
GVL	Graft Versus Leukemia effect
GY	GraY (measure of radiation)
GYN	GYNecology
H	Hours or Hydrogen or Hispanic or Heavy
HA	Headache or Hospital Admission
H1	Hypothesis alternative
H2	Histamine 2 receptor (receptor/target)
H2A	Histamine 2 Antagonists
H3	Histamine 3 receptor (receptor/target)
HAART	Highly Active Anti-Retroviral Therapy
HA1C	Hemoglobin A1C (glycosylated)
HAMA	Human Antibody to Murine Antibody
HAQ	Health Assessment Questionnaire
HAS	Hamilton Anxiety Scale
HAT	Histone AcetylTransferase (receptor/target) or Human AntiThrombin (receptor/target)
HAV	Hepatitis A Virus
HazDat	HAZardous substances release and health effects DATabase
HB	HemogloBin
HBA1	HemogloBin A 1 (glycosylated hemoglobin in blood)
HBCATC	Human Branched-Chain AminoTransferase Cytosolic (receptor/target)
HBV	Hepatitis B Virus
HC	High Concentration or Heavy Chain (Mab) or HydroCortisone
HCFA	Health Care Financing Administration
HCL	HydroChLoride or Hairy Cell Leukemia
HCP	Health Care Professional or Host Cell Proteins or Human CarboxyPeptidase (receptor/target)
HCPCS	Healthcare Common Procedural Coding System (J-codes, HCFA)
HCT	HematoCriT or HydroChloroThiazide

HCU	Health Care Utilization
HCV	Hepatitis C Virus
HD	High Dose or Hodgkin's Disease or HemoDialysis or Hospital Day or Half Dose
HDAC	Histone DeACetylase (-3, -7) enzyme (receptor/target)
HDC	High Dose Chemotherapy or Histidine DeCarboxylase (receptor/target)
HDL	High Density Lipoprotein
HDMTX	High Dose MethoTreXate, leucovorin (CA TX Sarcomas)
HDPE	High Density PolyEthylene
HDRS	Hamilton Depression Rating Scale
HE	Health Economics
HED	Human Equivalent Dose
HEENT	Head, Eyes, Ears, Nose, and Throat
HEDIS	Health plan Employer Data and Information Set
HER2	Human Epidermal growth factor Receptor 2 (receptor/target)
HG	HemoGlobin or mercury (symbol in elemental chart)
HGF	Hematopoietic Growth Factor
HGP	Human Genome Project
HGT	Human Genetic Therapies
HDMA	Healthcare Distribution Management Association
HemOnc	HEMatology and ONCology
HGH	Human Growth Hormone
HH	HedgeHog (receptor/target) or Hemoglobin and Hematocrit
HHS	Health and Human Services
HI	Health Insurance or HawaiI
HIF P	Hypoxia-Inducible Factor Protein (receptor/target)
HIPAA	Health Insurance Portability and Accountability Act
HIST	HISTamine (receptor/target)
HIS	HIStidine or HIStamine
HIT	Heparin-Induced Thrombocytopenia
HIV	Human Immune Virus

HLA	Human Leukocyte Antigen (receptor/target)
HLT	Hydroxy-LeukoTrienes (receptor/target)
HMG	HeMoGlobin
HMG-CoA	HydroxyMethylGlutaryl-CO-enzyme A (receptor/target)
HMO	Health Maintenance Organization
HMOX1	HaeMe OXygenase 1 (receptor/target)
HMPC	Herbal Medicine Products Committee (in Europe)
HN	Head and Neck or Head Nurse
HNC	Head and Neck Cancer
HNF	Hepatocytic Nuclear Factor-1 (receptor/target)
H$_o$	null Hypothesis
HO	House Officer
H2O	water
HP	High Potency or Hewlett-Packard (computer company) or History and Physical
HPI	History of Present Illness
HPLC	High Pressure Liquid Chromatography
HPPD	HydroxyPhenylPyruvate Dioxygenase (receptor/target)
HPT	HyPerTension
HPV	Human Papilloma Virus
HPW	Highly Purified Water
HQA	Hospital Quality Alliance (CMS group)
HR	Human Resources or Heart Rate or HouR
H1R	Histamine-1 Receptor (receptor/target)
H2R	Histamine-2 Receptor (receptor/target)
H3R	Histamine-3 Receptor (receptor/target)
HRD	Human Renal Dehydropeptidase (receptor/target)
HRG	Health Research Group (FDA/Public citizen group)
HRQOL	Health Related Quality Of Life
HRS	Hamilton Rating Scale
HRSA	Health Resources and Services Administration (in CMS)
HRT	Hormone Replacement Therapy or HeaRT
HS	Hora Somni (Latin for at bedtime) or Half Strength

HSA	Health Savings Account or Human Serum Albumin
HSD	3-beta-HydroxySteroid Dehydrogenase (receptor/target)
HSP	Human Subject Protection (Initiative of FDA) or Heat Shock Protein (receptor/target)
HSR	Health Services Research
HSV	Herpes Simplex Virus
HT	HeighT or HyroxyTryptamine (-1, -2, -3, -4, -5, -6, or -7) (receptor/ target) or HyperTension
5HT-1	Serotonin (-1A, -1B, -1D, -1F) (receptor/target)
5HT-2	Serotonin (-2A, -2B, -2C) (receptor/target)
5HT-4	Serotonin (4) (receptor/target)
HTA	Health Technology Assessments (in CMS)
HTCFA	Human Tumor Colony Forming Assay
HTN	HyperTensioN
HTS	High Throughput Screening
HUGO	HUman Genome Organization
HVAC	Heating, Ventilation, and Air Conditioning
HVP	High Volume Prescriber
HX	History
I	One (Roman numeral)
IAP	Inhibitor of Apoptosis Protein (receptor/target)
IB	Investigator's Brochure or Industrial Biotechnology or Irritable Bowel
IBD	Inflammatory Bowel Disease
IBQ	Illness Behavior Questionnaire
IBS	Irritable Bowel Syndrome
IBW	Ideal Body Weight
IC	Informed Consent or Intensive Care or Inter Cibum (Latin for between meals)
ICAAC	Interscience Conference for Antimicrobial Agents and Chemotherapy
IC50	Inhibitory Concentration at 50%
ICAM	Inhibiting Cell Adhesion Molecule (receptor/target)

ICC	Interstate Commerce Commission
ICD-9	International Classification of Disease, 9th revision
ICE	IL-1 Beta Converting Enzyme (receptor/target) or Iphosphamide, Carboplatin, Etoposide (CA CT Sarcoma)
ICF	Informed Consent Form or Intermediate Care Facility
ICH	International Conference on Harmonization (regulatory and research guidelines)
ICH E3	ICH guidance for final report writing
ICH E8	ICH guidance for clinical trials
ICH E9	ICH guidance for statistics in trials
ICH M3	ICH guidance for animal toxicology studies
ICH S1A	ICH guidance for carcinogenicity studies
ICMJE	International Committee of Medical Journal Editors
ICOS	Inducible t-cell CO-Stimulator ICU (receptor/target)
ICSR	Individual Case Safety Report
ICU	Intensive Care Unit (in a hospital)
ID	IntraDermal injection or IDentification or Infectious Disease or Iphosphamide, mesna, Doxorubicin (CA CT Sarcoma)
IDDM	Insulin-Dependent Diabetes Mellitus
IDE	Investigational Device Exemption
IDMC	Independent Data Monitoring Committee
IDSA	Infectious Disease Society of America
IE	Iphosphamide, Etoposide, mesna (CA CT Sarcoma) or Id Est (Latin for that is)
IEC	Independent Ethics Committee or Institutional Ethics Committee or Ion Exchange Chromatography
IES	Impact Event Scale
IFIC	International Food Information Council
IFN	InterFeroN
IFOVP	IFOsphamide, VePesid (CA CT Osteosarcoma)
IFPIA	International Federation of Pharmaceutical Industries and Associations
IFPMA	International Federation of Pharmaceutical Manufacturers and Associations

IG	ImmunoGlobulin (IgA, IgE, IgG, IgM)
IgA	Immunoglobulin-A
IgE	ImmunoGlobulin-E
IgG	ImmunoGlobulin-G
IgM	ImmunoGlobulin-M
IHC	ImmunoHistoChemistry
IHS	Integrated Health System or Indian Health Service
IIS	Investigator-Initiated Study
IIT	Investigator-Initiated Trial
IKK	Inhibitor of Kappa Kinase (receptor/target)
IL1RA	InterLeukin-1 Receptor Antagonist (receptor/target)
ILE	IsoLEucine
IL	InterLeukin
IL-1	InterLeukin (-1 up to -21) (receptor/target)
ILAK	InterLeukin-Associated Kinase (receptor/target)
ILSI	International Life Sciences Institute
IM	IntraMuscular injection or Information Management or Internal Medicine
IMAC	Iphosphamide, Mesna, Adriamycin, Cisplatin (CA CT Sarcoma)
IMI	Innovative Medicines Initiative (EU program for research collaboration of academia, companies, and regulators)
IMF	Iphosphamide, mesna, Methotrexate, Fluorouracil (CA CT Breast)
IMP	Inosine- (or -4) MonoPhosphatase (receptor/target)
IMP DHG	Inosine-5-MonoPhosphate DeHydroGenase (-1, -2) (receptor/target)
IMS	Institute for Medical Sciences (Drug marketing and sales data)
IMVP-16	Iphosphamide, Mesna, Methotrexate, Vepesid (CA CT NHL)
IN	IntraNasal or INch or INdiana
IN-111	INidium-111 (radioactive nuclide)
INAD	Investigational New Animal Drug
INC	INCorporated or INComplete or INCrease

INCB	International Narcotics Control Board (with United Nations)
IND	Investigational New Drug application (to FDA)
INF	INterFerons or Inhibitor of Nuclear Factor kappa b kinase (receptor/target)
INR	International Normalized Ratio (for PT comparisons)
INS	INSurance or Immigration and Naturalization Service or INSulin (receptor/target)
I&O	Input and Output (as in fluids for a patient)
IOM	Institute of Medicine
IOP	IntraOcular Pressure
IP	IntraPeritoneal or IntraPulmonary or IntraPleural or Intellectual Property or Investigational Plan or Isoelectric Point
IP3	Inositol 1, 4, 5-triPhosphate (receptor/target)
IPC	In-Process Control (changes in manufacturing)
IPEC	International Pharmaceutical Excipients Council
IPO	Initial Public Offering (for sale of stock)
IPPB	Intermittent Positive Pressure Breathing
IPPI	Inositol Polyphosphate Phosphatase Inhibitor (receptor/target)
IPPS	Inpatient Prospective Payment System (for Medicare drugs)
IPSS	International Prognostic Scoring System
IQ	Intelligence Quotient
IQWiG	Institute for Quality and Cost Effectiveness in Healthcare System (in Germany)
IR	Investor Relations or Immediate Release or Information Request letter (from FDA) or Investigator Recruitment or Insulin Receptor (receptor/target) or Investigator Reports
IRA	Individual Retirement Account
IRB	Institutional Review Board
IRC	Internal Revenue Code (in USA)
IRIN	Integrated Regional Information Network (with the United Nations)

IRR	Internal Rate of Return
IRS	Internal Revenue Service or Insulin Receptor Substrate (receptor/target)
IS	Information Systems or Investigative Sites
ISA	Instrumentation, Systems, and Automation society
ISMP	Institute for Safe Medication Practices
ISPE	International Society of Pharmaceutical Engineering
ISR	International Search Report (for patents)
ISO	International Organization for Standardization
ISO 1401	Certification of environmental impact and compliance (in Europe)
ISO 9000	Quality program(s) for excellence for processes in a company
ISPE	International Society of Pharmaceutical Engineers
IST	Investigator-Sponsored Trial
IT	Information Technology or IntraThecal injection or ImmunoTherapy or ITaly or Inhalation Therapy
ITC	International Trade Commission
ITD	IodoThyronine Deiodinase (receptor/target)
ITK	Il-2 inducible T-cell Kinase (receptor/target)
ITP	Idiopathic Thrombocytopenic Purpura
ITT	Intent-To-Treat (group of patients in a clinical trial)
IU	International Unit or Indiana University
IUCAC	Institutional Animal Care and Use Committee
IUD	Intra-Uterine Device
IV	IntraVenous injection or IntraVentricular injection or In Vitro or In Vivo or four (in Latin)
IVD	In Vitro Diagnostics
IVF	In Vitro Fertilization
IVP	IntraVenous Push
IVRS	Interactive Voice Response System
IWG	International Working Group
J	Joule
JAFAS	Juvenile Arthritis Functional Assessment Scale

JAK	JAnus Kinase (-1, -2 or -3) (receptor/target)
JAMA	the Journal of the American Medical Association
JCAHO	Joint Commission on Accreditation of Healthcare Organization (currently known as Joint Commission)
JCP	Journal of Clinical Pharmacology
JCPP	Joint Commission of Pharmacy Practitioners
JD	Juris Doctor (lawyer)
JEV	Japanese Encephalitis Virus
J&J	Johnson and Johnson, Inc.
JNK	Jun N-terminal Kinase (receptor/target)
JNC 7	Joint National Committee (for cardiovascular disorders)
JPMA	Japan Pharmaceutical Manufacturers Association
JR	JunioR
JRA	Juvenile Rheumatoid Arthritis
JT	JoinT
JV	Joint Venture
Jx	Juncture

K	Thousand (Latin numeral; as in dollars or items) or constants in scientific formulas or potassium (in elemental chart) or Kelvin (temperature scale) or Kilo
KA	KetoAcidosis
KAI	Kirton Adaptation-Innovation inventory
KC	Keratinocyte-derived Chemokine (receptor/target)
Kv	Potassium Voltage channel receptor (receptor/target)
K-CR	Potassium Channel Receptor (receptor/target)
kD	KiloDalton (measure of molecular weight)
KG	KiloGram
Km	substrate binding affinity for a compound
KM	Kaplan-Meier
KO	Knock-Out (as in gene KOs in mice) or Keep Open
KOL	Key Opinion Leaders
KOR	Keep Open Rate (in parenteral administration) or Kappa Opioid Receptor (receptor/target)
Kow	solubility constant for a substance in water

KPs	Key Prescribers
KPI	Key Performance Indicator
KPS	Karnofsky Performance Status
KRA	Key Results Areas
KS	Kaposi's Sarcoma or KanSas
L	Liter or fifty (Roman numeral) or Left or Lung or Liver or Light or Lower or Ligand or Liter
LA	Long Acting (formulation) or Licensing and Acquisitions or Latin-American or Los Angeles
LAIV	Live Attenuated Influenza Vaccines
LAM	Leukocyte Adhesion Molecule (receptor/target)
LASA	Linear Analog Scale Assessment
LAT	LATeral or Linker for Activation of T-cells (receptor/target)
LB	pound (in English currency)
LBM	Lean Body Mass
LBO	Leveraged Buy-Out
LC	Liquid Chromatography (in drug analysis) or Light Chain (Mab)
LCD	Local Coverage Determination (in DHHS)
LCM	Life Cycle Management or Laser Capture Microdissection
LCSS	Lung Cancer Symptom Scale
LCT	Long Chain Triglycerides
LD50	Lethal Dose in 50% (of animals in toxicology studies)
LDH	Lactic DeHydrogenase (receptor/target)
LDL	Low Density Lipoprotein
LE	Latest Estimate (of sales or expenses or budget, etc.) or Lupus Erythematosus or Left Eye
LEU	LEUcine
LFA	Lymphocyte Function-associated Antigen (receptor/target)
LFT	Liver Function Test
LHRH	Leuteinizing Hormone Releasing Hormone (receptor/target)

LIF	Leukemia Inhibitory Factor (receptor/target)
LIQ	LIQuid
LLC	Limited Liability Corporation
LMD	Local Medical Doctor
LMWH	Low Molecular Weight Heparin
5LO	5-LipoOxygenase (receptor/target)
LOAEL	Lowest Observed Adverse Effect Level
LOI	Letter Of Intent
LOS	Length Of Stay (in hospital)
LOX	LipoOXygenase (receptor/target)
LP	Limited Partnership or Lumbar Puncture or Liquid Pressure
LPA	LipoPeptide Antibiotics
LPL	LipoProtein Lipase (receptor/target)
LPLV	Last Patient Last Visit
LPN	Licensed Practical Nurse
LPS	LipoPolySaccharide (receptor/target)
LR	Lactated Ringers (solution) or Legal and Regulatory (Departments)
LRP	Long Range Plan
LSE	Last Subject Enrolled
LSP	Life Skills Profile
LST	Large Simple Trials
LT	LeukoTriene (-B, -D, or -E) (receptor/target) or LefT
LTC	Long-Term Care
LTCF	Long-Term Care Facility
LTCI	Long-Term Care Insurance
LTD	LimiTeD (as in a company or business organization in Europe)
LTR	LymphoToxin Receptor (receptor/target) or LiTeR
LVEF	Left Ventricular Ejection Fraction
LVH	Left Ventricular Hypertrophy
LVAM	Leuprolide, Vinblastine, Adriamycin, Mitomycin C (CA CT GU)
LVN	Licensed Vocational Nurse

LVP	Large Volume Parenterals
LYS	LYSine
LX	LuXury

M	Male or Million or Meter or Mile or Married or Muscarinic (-1, -2, -3, -4, or -5) (receptor/target) or Murmur or Milli- or Mass or Month or Mother
M2	Melphalan, Oncovin, Carmustine, Cyclophosphamide, Prednisone (CA CT MM)
MA	Medical Affairs or Medicare Advantage (service regions for Medicare Part D drug program) or Marketing Authorization (in European Union) or Meta-Analysis or MicroArray or Medical Authorization or Master of Arts (degree)
MAA	Medicines Authorization Application (to European regulatory agency)
M&A	Mergers and Acquisitions
MAB	Monoclonal AntiBody
MABEL	Minimum Active Biological Effect Level
MAC	Maximum Allowable Cost or Maximum Allowable Concentration
MACC	Methotrexate, Adriamycin, Cyclophosphamide, CeeNU (CA CT NSCLC)
MACOP-B	Methotrexate, Adriamycin, Cyclophosphamide, Oncovin, Prednisolone, Bleomycin, leucovorin (CA CT NHL)
MADRS	Montgomery-Asberg Depression Rating Scale
MAH	Marketing Authorization Holder (in EU)
MAID	Mesna, Adriamycin, Iphosphamide, Dacarbazine (CA CT Sarcoma)
MAM	Marketing Area Manager
MANOVA	Multiple ANalysis Of VAriance
MAO-B	MonoAmine Oxidase B (receptor/target)
MAOI	MonoAmine Oxidase Inhibitor (receptor/target)
MAP	Mean Arterial Pressure or Mitomycin C, Adriamycin, Platinol (CA CT HN)

MAPD	Medicare Advantage Prescription Drug
MAPK	Mitogen-Activated Protein Kinase (receptor/target)
MaPP	Manual of Policies and Procedures (in FDA)
MAQC	MicroArray Quality Control
M-AR	Muscarinic (-1, -2, -3, -4, or -5) Acetylcholine Receptors (receptor/target)
MB	Medical Bachelors (degree for medicine in Europe) or Myers Briggs inventory
MBA	Masters in Business Administration
mBACOD	Bleomycin, Adriamycin, Cyclophosphamide, Oncovin, Dexamethasone, leucovorin (CA CT NHL)
MBC	Methotrexate, Bleomycin, Cisplatin (CA CT HN) or Minimum Bacterial Concentration
MC	Medical Communications or Masters of Ceremony or Medicinal Chemistry or MelanoCortin peptides (receptor/target) or MultiCenter
MCB	Master Cell Bank
MCG	MiCroGram
MCHR	Melanin-Concentrating Hormone Receptor (receptor/target)
MCO	Managed Care Organization
MCR	MelanoCortin Receptor (receptor/target) or MineraloCorticoid Receptor (receptor/target)
MCS	Multi-Center Study
MCSF	Macrophage Colony-Stimulating Factor (receptor/target)
MCV	Mean Corpuscular Volume
MCWB	Master Cell Working Bank
MD	Medical Doctor or Muscular Dystrophy or Medical Director or Manic Depression or Marketing Director
MDD	Mean Droplet Diameter or Major Depressive Disorder
MDI	Metered Dose Inhaler or Major Depression Inventory
MDR	Multiple Drug Resistance or Minimum Daily Requirement
MDS	MyeloDysplastic Syndrome
MDUFMA	Medical Device User Fee Modernization Act

MDV	MultiDose Vial
ME	Molecular Engineering or Medical Examiner
MEC	Minimum Effective Concentration
MeCP	Methyl-CCNU, Cyclophosphamide, Prednisone (CA CT MM)
MED	Minimum Effective Dose or Minimum Erythemal Dose or Maximum Effective Dose or Maximum Erythemal Dose or MEDication or Medical Education Department or Masters in Education or MEDial
MedDRA	Medical Dictionary for Regulatory Activities (terms for coding adverse events in reports)
Med Hx	Medical History
MEDPAC	MEDicaid Payment Advisory Commission
MEK	Mitogen activated protein Kinase (receptor/target)
MEMS	MicroElectroMagnetic Systems
MEP	Manufacturing Extension Partnership (in NIH)
MEQ	MilliEQuivalent
MERS	Model Errors Reporting System
MET	METhionine
METS	METastaseS (in cancer)
MF	Methotrexate, Fluorouracil, leucovorin (CA CT HN)
MG	MilliGram or MaGnesium or Myasthenia Gravis
MGA	Maltase GlucoAmylase (receptor/target)
MGLUR	Metabotropic GLUtamate Receptor (receptor/target)
MH	Mental Health
MHC	Major Histocompatability Complex (receptor/target)
MHI	Mental Health Inventory
MHIQ	Mental Health Index Questionnaire
MHLW	Ministry of Health, Labor, and Welfare (in Japan)
MHRA	Medicines and Healthcare products Regulatory Agency (in United Kingdom)
MHX	Medical History
MI	Medical Information or MIle or Myocardial Infarction or MIchigan
MIAMI	Microarray Integrated Analysis of Methylation by Isoschizomers

MIC	Minimum Inhibitory Concentration
MICE	Mesna, Ifosfamide, Carboplatin, Etoposide (CA CT NSCLC)
MICU	Medical Intensive Care Unit
MIF	Migration Inhibitory Factor (receptor/target)
MIN	MINutes or MINimum
MINE	Mesna, Ifosfamide, Novantrone, Etoposide (CA CT NHL)
MIP	Management Incentive Plan (bonus plan) or Macrophage Inhibitory Protein (receptor/target)
MIRNA	MicroInhibitory RNA
MKI	MultiKinase Inhibitor (receptor/target)
ML	MilliLiter or MiLe
MLD	Minimal Lethal Dose
MLP	Maximum Lifespan Potential
MLT	MeLaTonin (receptor/target) or MiLiTary
MLV	Multimellar Large Vesicles
MM	Millions (as in dollars) or MilliMeter or Medicare and Medicaid or Malignant Melanoma or Multiple Myeloma or Mercaptopurine, Methotrexate (CA CT ALL) or Morbidity and Mortality or MilliMoles or Marketing Manager
MMA	Medicare prescription drug, improvement, and Modernization Act (2003)
MMP	Matrix MetalloProteinase (receptor/target)
MMPI	Minnesota Multiphasic Personality Inventory
MMR	Morbidity and Mortality Reports (of the CDC) or Mumps Measles Rubella (vaccine) or MisMatch Repair (gene mutations)
MMS	Medicare and Medicaid Services (for U.S. government health agency)
MMSE	Mini-Mental State Examination
MMT	Medicare Management of Therapy program
MMV	Medicines for Malaria Venture
MMWR	Morbidity and Mortality Weekly Report (from CDC)
MO	Modus Operandi (the methods by which work is done) or Medical Officer or Mu Opioid receptor (receptor/target) or Medical Oncology

MOA	Mechanism of Action
MOMP	Mitochondrial Outer Membrane Permeabilization (receptor/target)
MOPP	Mechlorethamine, Oncovin, Procarbazine, Prednisone (CA CT Hodgkin's lymphoma or Brain CA)
MOS	Medication Outcomes Study
Motif	Structural feature of a product
MOU	Memorandum-Of-Understanding (from FDA for new regulations outside of written guidances or regulations) or Method Of Use (in patents)
MP	Melphalan, Prednisone (CA CT MM) or Military Police
MPH	Masters in Public Health
MPQ	McGill Pain Questionnaire
MPTP	1-Methyl-4-Phenyl-1,2,3,6-TetrahydroPyridine
MPK	Metabolism and PharmacoKinetics
MR	Market Research or Medical Record or MisteR or Mental Retardation or Melatonin Receptor (-1A, -1B) (receptor/target) or Mineralocorticoid Receptor (receptor/target) or Mutual Recognition (European Union drug approvals)
MRA	Medical Reimbursement Account or Mutual Recognition Agreements (in Europe among member states) or Muscarinic Receptor Agonists (receptor/target) or Muscarinic Receptor Antagonists (receptor/target)
MRE	Molecular Recognition Entity
MRI	Magnetic Resonance Imaging
MRFG	Mutual Recognition Facilitation Group (in Europe for EMEA)
MRLs	Maximum Residue Limits (in animals in Europe) or Minimum Risk Levels
MRP	Mutual Recognition Procedure (in European Union) or Medication Related Problem or Multiple Resistance-associated Protein (receptor/target)
MRSD	Maximum Recommended Starting Dose
MSQ	Mental Status Questionnaire

MRSA	Methicillin-Resistant Staphylococcus Aureus
MRT	Mean Residence Time
MS	Mass Spectrophotometry (in drug analysis) or Modeling and Simulation (pharmacokinetic research in drug development) or Master of Science or Market Share or MisS (female single person) or Multiple Sclerosis or Medical Services or Morphine Sulphate
MSC	Maximum Safe Concentration
MSAs	Medical Savings Account or Metropolitan Statistical Areas
MSF	Medecins Sans Frontieres (Doctors Without Borders)
MSH	Melanocyte Stimulating Hormone (receptor/target)
MSK	MusculoSKeletal or Memorial Sloan Kettering (hospital)
MSL	Medical Science Liaison
MSM	Medical Science Manager
MST	Mountain Standard Time (United States)
MTA	Materials Transfer Agreement (with NIH)
MTC	Maximum Tolerated Concentration
MTD	Maximum Tolerated Dose
MTM	Medication Therapy Management
MTMP	Medication Therapy Management Program
MTMS	Medication Therapy Management Services
mTORR	mammalian Target Of Rapamycin Receptor (receptor/target)
MUE	Morbidity Utilization Evaluation or Medication Utilization Review
MUNJI	Multi-Use Nozzle Jet Injector
MUS	Medication Use Safety
MV	MultiVitamin or Mitoxantrone, Vepesid (CA CT AML)
MVA	MultiVariate Analysis
MVAC	Methotrexate, Vinblastine, Adriamycin, Cisplatin (CA CT GU)
MVD	MicroVessel Density
MVI	MultiVitamin Infusion
MVPP	Mechlorethamine, Vinblastine, Procarbazine, Prednisone (CA CT Hodgkin's lymphoma)

MW	Medical Writing or Molecular Weight
MWCB	Master Working Cell Bank
MWT	Molecular WeighT
MYD88	MYeloid Differentiation primary response gene

N	Number (of subjects in a study) or No or Normal or Negative or Nano or North
NA	National Accounts or Nucleic Acid or Not Available or NorAdrenaline (receptor/target) or Navelbine, Adriamycin (CA CT Breast) or North America or Not Applicable or Not Approvable (of NDA by FDA)
NAAMECC	North American Association of Medical Education and Communication Companies
NAB	National Advisory Board or Neutralizing AntiBody
NABP	National Association of Boards of Pharmacy
nAChR	n-AcetylCholine Receptor (receptor/target)
NA-CR	Sodium-Channel Receptor (receptor/target)
NAD	No Appreciable Disease or No Acute Distress
NADA	New Animal Drug Application
NADP	Nicotinamide Adenine Dinucleotide Phosphate (receptor/target)
NAFTA	North American Free Trade Agreement
NAMCS	National Ambulatory Medication Care Survey
NARD	National Association of Retail Druggists
NAS	National Academy of Sciences or New Active Substance
NAT	N-AcetylTransferase (receptor/target)
NaV	Sodium Voltage channel receptor (receptor/target)
NB	New Born or National Brand
NBAC	National Bioethics Advisory Commission
NBD	New Business Development
NBME	National Board of Medical Examiners
NBRA	National Biotechnology Regulatory Authority (in India)
NBT	NanoBioTechnology
NC	Non-Clinical (data or study) or No Charge or No Change or North Carolina

NCBI	National Center for Biotechnology Information (U.S. NLM and NIH)
NCIC	National Cancer Institute of Canada
NCI CTC	National Cancer Institute Common Toxicity Criteria
NCCN	National Comprehensive Cancer Network
NCCTG	North Central Cancer Treatment Group
NCD	National Coverage Determination (by CMS)
NCE	New Chemical Entity
NCEP	National Cholesterol Expert Panel
NCGC	National Chemical Genomics Center
NCHS	National Center for Health Statistics (in CMS)
NCI	National Cancer Institute (in NIH)
NCID	National Center for Infectious Diseases
NCMHD	National Center on Minority Health and Health Disparities (in NIH)
NCPA	National Community Pharmacists Association
NCQA	National Committee for Quality Assurance
NCR	NociCeption Receptor (receptor/target)
NCRR	National Center for Research Resources (in NIH)
NCTS	National Center for Toxicological Research (in FDA)
ND	Not Done or North Dakota or Not Determined or No Disease
NDA	New Drug Application or Non-Disclosure Agreement
NDC	National Drug Code
NDR	Non-Drug Related
NDTI	National Disease and Therapeutic Index
NE	NorEpinephrine (receptor/target) or New England or No Effect
NED	No Evidence of Disease
NEJM	New England Journal of Medicine
NEP	Neutral EndoPeptidase (receptor/target)
NET	NorEpinephrine Transporter (receptor/target)
NF	National Formulary or Nuclear Factor (receptor/target) or Not Found
NF-KB	Nuclear Factor Kappa Beta (receptor/target)
NFL	Novantrone, Fluorouracil, Leucovorin (CA CT Breast)

NFS	Not For Sale
NG	NanoGram or NitroGlycerin
NGF	Nerve Growth Factor (receptor/target)
NGR	NoGo Receptor (nerve growth) (receptor/target)
NH	Nursing Home or New Hampshire
NHCS	National Health Care Survey (by CDC)
NHE	National Health Expenditures
NHF	National Headache Foundation
NHGRI	National Human Genome Research Institute (In NIH)
NHI	National Health Insurance program (in Japan)
NHIS	National Health Interview Survey
NHL	Non-Hodgkin's Lymphoma
NHLBI	National Heart Lung and Blood Institute (in NIH)
NHMA	National Hispanic Medical Association
NHP	Natural Health Products or Nottingham Health Profile
NHS	National Heath Service (in United Kingdom)
NIA	National Institute on Aging (in NIH)
NIAAA	National Institute on Alcohol Abuse and Alcoholism (in NIH)
NIAID	National Institute of Allergy and Infectious Disease (in NIH)
NIAMS	National Institute of Arthritis, Musculoskeletal and Skin Diseases (in NIH)
NIBIB	National Institute of Biomedical Imaging and Bioengineering (in NIH)
NIBR	Novartis Institute for Biomedical Research
NICE	National Institute for Health and Clinical Excellence (in United Kingdom)
NICHD	National Institute of Child Health and Human Development (in NIH)
NIDA	National Institute of Drug Abuse (in NIH)
NIDDK	National Institute of Diabetes and Digestive and Kidney Diseases (in NIH)
NIDDM	Non-Insulin Dependent Diabetes Mellitus

NIDP	Notice of Initiation of Disqualification Proceedings (with FDA)
NIEHS	National Institute of Environmental Health Sciences
NIGMS	National Institute of General Medical Sciences
NIH	National Institutes of Health
NIMH	National Institute of Mental Health (in NIH)
NINDS	National Institute of Neurologic Disorders and Stroke (in NIH)
NINR	National Institute of Nursing Research (in NIH)
NIOSH	National Institute for Occupational Safety and Health (in NIH)
NIPCO	National Institute for Pharmacist Care Outcomes
NIST	National Institute of Standards and Technology
NK	tachyKinins (receptor/target) or NeuroKinin-1 (receptor/target)
NK3	NeuroKinase 3 receptor (receptor/target)
NK cell	Natural Killer cell (receptor/target)
NKF	National Kidney Foundation
NL	NormaL
NLM	National Library of Medicine (United States)
NLR	Nod-Like Receptor (receptor/target)
NLRN	National Library Response Network (in CDC for bioterrorism)
NLT	Not Less Than
NM	NeuroMuscular or Not Mentioned
NMA	National Medical Association
NMDA	N-Methyl-D-Aspartate sensitive glutamate receptors (receptor/target)
NME	New Molecular Entity
NMMLSC	New Mexico Molecular Libraries Screening Center
NMR	Nuclear Magnetic Resonance
NMSS	National Multiple Sclerosis Society
NNRTI	Non-Nucleoside Reverse Transcriptase Inhibitor (receptor/target)
NNT	Number Needed to Treat
NO	Nitric Oxide (receptor/target) or NeuroOncology

NOAEL	NO Adverse Effect Level (for dosing in animal studies)
NOEL	No Observable Effect Level
NOF	National Osteoporosis Foundation
NOGA	Notice Of Grant Award (from NIH)
NORD	National Organization for Rare Diseases
NOS	Nitric Oxide Synthase (receptor/target)
NOSIE	Nurses' Observation In-patient Evaluation
NOV	Notice of Violation (letter from FDA DDMAC)
NOVP	Novantrone, Oncovin, Vinblastine, Prednisone (CA CT NHL)
NP	Nurse Practitioner or NeuroPeptides (receptor/target) or Not Present or No Pain or NucleoProtein (receptor/target)
NPDB	National Practitioner Data Bank (in HHS)
NPC	National Pharmaceutical Council
NPE	Nominal Price Exemption (in Medicaid drug rebate program)
NPF	National Parkinson Foundation
NPH	Neutral Protamine Hagedorn (for insulin)
NPI	National Provider Identifier (number from CMS) or No Present Illness
NPO	Non Per Os (Latin for nothing by mouth)
NPPA	National Pharmaceutical Pricing Authority (in UK)
NPRA	Natriuretic Peptide Receptor A (receptor/target)
NPS	National Provider System (CMS system for NPIs)
NPSF	National Patient Safety Foundation
NPV	Net Present Value
NPY	NeuroPeptide Y (receptor/target)
NQF	National Quality Forum
NR	No Risk or Not Rated or Not Reported or No Refills or Normal Range
N3R	Nuclear-3 Receptor (-4) (receptor/target)
NRC	Nuclear Regulatory Commission
NRG	Name Review Group (in European Union, EMEA)
NRDO	No Research Development Only (type of company)
NRPS	NonRibosomal Peptide Synthetase (receptor/target)

NRSA	National Research Service Award (by NIH)
NRTI	Nucleotide Reverse Transcriptase Inhibitor (receptor/target)
NS	Normal Saline or Not Significant
NSA	National Stroke Association or National Security Administration or Normal Serum Albumin
NSABP	National Surgical Adjuvant Breast and Bowel Project
NSD	Not Significantly Different
NSAIA	Non-Steroidal Anti-Inflammatory Agent
NSAID	Non-Steroidal Anti-Inflammatory Drug
NSC	number from National Service Center (of NCI for cancer chemotherapy products) or No Significant Change
NSCLC	Non-Small Cell Lung Cancer
NSF	National Science Foundation
NSRI	Non-Selective serotonin Reuptake Inhibitor (receptor/target)
NSS	Neurotransmitter Sodium Symporter family (receptor/target)
NT	Not Tested or NeuroTensin (receptor/target) or NeuroTrophins (receptor/target) or Normal Temperature or No Treatment
NTAL	Non-T-cell Activator Linker (receptor/target)
NT3	NeuroTrophic Factor-3 (receptor/target)
NTP	National Toxicology Program (in HHS)
NTSN	NeuroTenSiN (receptor/target)
NUNT	Adenosine and Uridine Triphosphates (receptor/target)
NV	Normal Value or Nausea and Vomiting
NOVP	Novantrone, Oncovin, Vinblastine, Prednisone (CA TX HD)
NYHA	New York Heart Association
O	Oral or Objective or Orphan (review classification of FDA for NDA)
O2	Oxygen
OA	OsteoArthritis

OAI	Official Action Indicated (FDA letter to company)
OB	OBstetrics
OBBR	Office of Blood Research Review (in FDA)
OBP	Office of Biotechnology Products (in FDA)
OBQI	Oncology Biomarker Quality Initiative (with FDA-NIH-CMS)
OBRA	Omnibus Budget Reconciliation Act (1990)
OBS	OBServed
OC	Operating Costs or Oral Contraceptives or Ovarian Cancer or On Call
OCD	Obsessive Compulsive Disorder
OCP	Office of Combination Products (in FDA)
OCSQ	Office of Clinical Standards and Quality (in CMS)
OCTGT	Office of Cellular, Tissue, and Gene Therapies (in FDA)
OD	Oculo Dextro (Latin for right eye) or OverDose
ODA	Orphan Drug Act (1983)
ODAC	Oncology Drug Advisory Committee (for FDA)
ODC	Ornithine DeCarboxylate (receptor/target)
ODE	Office of Drug Evaluation (-I through -VI in FDA)
ODM	Optional Data Model
ODN	OligoDeoxyNucleotide (receptor/target)
ODS	Office of Drug Safety (in FDA)
ODT	Orally Disintegrating Tablet
OECD	Office for Economic Cooperation and Development
OEP	Office of Executive Programs (in FDA)
OER	Office of Extramural Research (in FDA or NIH)
OFT	Office of Fair Trade (in United Kingdom)
OGD	Office of Generic Drugs (in FDA)
OHRP	Office of Human Research Protections (in CMS)
OIG	Office of Inspector General (in Justice Department)
OK	all right
OL	Oculo Laevo (Latin for left eye) or Open Label
OLF	OLFactory
OLIGOS	OLIGOnucleotideS (receptor/target)
OM	Office of Management (in FDA)

OMB	Office of Management and Budget (in U.S. Congress)
ONs	OligoNucleotides
ONADE	Office of New Animal Drug Evaluation (in FDA)
ONDC	Office of New Drug Chemistry (in FDA)
OODD	Office of Orphan Drug Division (in FDA)
OOP	Out-Of-Pocket (expenses paid by patients outside of Medicare or insurance coverage)
OOS	Out Of Specification (FDA designation for product outside of specifications or accepted criteria in an NDA)
OP	OrthoPedics or OsteoPorosis or OPioids (receptor/target) or OPeration or OutPatients or Operating Profits or Office of Planning (of FDA)
OPA	Oncovin, Prednisone, Adriamycin (CA CT Lymphoma)
OPC	Official Package Circular (package insert) or OutPatient Clinic
OPD	Out-Patient Departments (of hospitals) or Orphan Product Development or Office of Orphan Product Development (in FDA)
OPDRA	Office of Post-marketing Drug Risk Assessment (in FDA)
OPEN	Oncovin, Prednisone, Etoposide, Novantrone (CA TX NHL)
OPH	OPHthalmic
OPL	OPinion Leader
OPPA	Oncovin, Procarbazine, Prednisone, Adriamycin (CA CT Lymphoma)
OPPS	Outpatient Prospective Payment System (for Medicare drugs)
OPRR	Office for the Protection from Research Risks (in FDA)
OPS	Office of Pharmaceutical Science (in FDA) or OutPatientS or Option Pricing Analysis
OPSS	Office of Pharmacoepidemiology and Statistical Science (in FDA)
OPT	Office of Pediatric Therapeutics (in FDA)
OQ	Operational Qualification
OR	Operating Room or Odds Ratio or Overall Risk or Opioid Receptor (-mu, -kappa, -delta) (receptor/target)

ORA	Office of Regulatory Affairs (in FDA)
ORDI	Office of Research, Development, and Information (in CMS)
ORF	Open Reading Frame (in genome analysis)
ORR	Overall Response Rate
OS	Out-Sourcing or Overall Survival or Oculo Sinistro (Latin for both eyes)
OSCHR	Office for Strategic Coordination of Health Research (in United Kingdom)
OSE	Office of Safety Evaluation (in FDA) or Office of Surveillance and Epidemiology (in FDA)
OSHA	Office of Safety and Health Administration
OSORA	Office of Strategic Operations and Regulatory Affairs (in CMS)
OSR	Office of Sponsored Research (in FDA)
OSS	Office of Share Services (in FDA)
OT	Over Time or On-Time or Occupational Therapy or OxyTocin agonists (receptor/target) or OxyTocin antagonists (receptor/target)
OTA	Office of Technology Assessment (in U.S. government) or OxyTocin Agonists (receptor/target)
OTC	Over-The-Counter
OTMC	Office of Technology Management and Communication
ORT	Office of Radiological Therapeutics (in FDA)
OTT	Office of Technology Transfer
OU	Oculo Utro (Latin for each eye)
OUR	Oxygen Uptake Rate
OV	Office Visit or OVarian
OVRR	Office of Vaccine Research and Review (in FDA)
OXM	OXyntoModulin
OXY	OXYtocin
OZ	Ounce
P	Probability (of an occurrence of an event in statistics) or Plan or Pressure or Priority (review classification of FDA for NDA)

3Ps	Patients, Providers, and Payers (Customers)
4Ps	Product, Place, Price, and Promotion (in marketing products)
8Ps	People, Pipeline, Processes, Profits, Principles, Performance, Portfolio, and Products (drug development needs and framework)
P.0	Phase 0 (research for early human studies at microdoses to examine safety and pharmacokinetics)
P.1	Phase 1 (clinical trial, usually normal subjects, pharmacokinetic and safety tests)
P.2	Phase 2 (clinical trial, patients with target disease, proof of concept study)
P.3	Phase 3 (pivotal clinical trial, establish safety and efficacy)
P.4	Phase 4 (post-marketing clinical trials)
P53	gene for tumor suppression (receptor/target)
P rating	Priority (review rating for new drug applications by FDA)
PA	Physician's Assistant or Prior Authorization or Prior Approval or Purchase Agreement or Posterior-Anterior or Pulmonary Artery or Program Announcement (from NIH) or Professional Association or Platelet Aggregation
PAA	Pancreatic Alpha-Amylase (receptor/target)
PABA	ParaAminoBenzoic Acid
PAC	Premature Atrial Contraction or Platinol, Adriamycin, Cyclophosphamide (CA TX OC) or Political Action Committee or Procaspase Activity Compound (receptor/target)
PACA	Pituitary Adenylate Cyclase-Activating peptide (receptor/target)
PAC–ATLS	Post-Approval Changes to NDA regarding Analytical Testing LaboratorieS
PAD	Peripheral Artery Disease or Pulmonary Arterial Disease or Pain And Depression scale or Pharmacologically Active Dose
PAER	Periodic Adverse Event Report

PAF	Platelet Activating Factor (receptor/target)
PAH	Pulmonary Arterial Hypertension
PAHO	Pan American Health Organization
PAI	PreApproval Inspection (by FDA)
P&G	Proctor and Gamble company
PAMP	Pathogen-Associated Molecular Patterns (receptor/target)
PAN-DRAH	Pan American Network of Drug Regulatory Harmonization
PAP	Prior Authorization Program or Patient Assistance Programs
PAR	Protease Activated Receptor (receptor/target) or an acceptable level of performance at average level or Proven Acceptable Ranges or Peri-Approval Research
PARP	Poly ADP-Ribose Polymerase (receptor/target)
PART	Program Assessment Rating Tool (in FDA)
PAS	Prior Approval Supplement
PASI	Psoriasis Area and Severity Index
PAT	Process Analytical Technology (initiative by FDA) or Paroxysmal Atrial Tachycardia
PB	Protein Bound or Peripheral Blood or Lead (in elemental chart)
PBM	Pharmacy Benefits Management (organization)
PBO	PlaceBO
PBPC	Peripheral Blood Progenitor Cell
PBPK	Physiologically Based PharmacoKinetics
PC	Placebo Control or PhysicoChemical or Pre-Clinical or Product Complaints or Primary Care or Patient Consent or Personal Computer or Pediatric Committee (E.U. group) or Post Cibum (Latin for after meals) or Paclitaxel, Carboplatin (CA CT GU) or Paclitaxel, Cisplatin (CA CT NSCLC) or PhosphatidylCholine (receptor/target)
PCA	Patient Controlled Analgesia or Principal Component Analysis
PCC	Poison Control Center or Product Complaint Center

PCF	Patient Consent Form
PCI	PerCutaneous Infusion or Percutaneous Coronary Intervention or Partial Cranial Irradiation
PCIR	Potassium Channel Inwardly Rectifying (receptor/target)
PCM	Project Control Manager
PCMA	Pharmaceutical Care Management Association
PCN	PeniCilliN
PCP	Primary Care Physician or Primary Care Providers
PCR	Polymerase Chain Reaction (in gene replication and expansion) or Principal Component Regression
PCT	Placebo-Controlled Trial or Patent Cooperation Treaty or Primary Care Trusts (in United Kingdom for reimbursement)
PCV	Procarbazine, Carmustine, Vincristine (CA TX Glioma)
PCWP	Pulmonary Capillary Wedge Pressure
PD	PharmacoDynamics or Progressive Disease or Peripheral Disease or Peritoneal Dialysis or Process Development or Parkinson's Disease or Product Development
PDA	Parenteral Drug Association or Personal Data Assistant
PDE	PhosphoDiEsterase, -1 up to -11 (receptor/target)
PDEI	PhosphoDiEsterase Inhibitors (receptor/target)
PDF	Portable Document Format
PDGF	Platelet Derived Growth Factor (alpha or beta) (receptor/target)
PDIT	PeDiatric Implementation Team (FDA cross-functional team in pediatrics evaluating PPSRs and WRs)
PDL	Preferred Drug List (for Medicare, Medicaid, or Insurers)
PDMA	Prescription Drug Marketing Act
PDP	Prescription Drug Plan (part of Medicare drug plan, Part D)
PDQ	Physician's Data Query (with NCI)
PDR	Physicians Desk Reference
PDRM	Preventable Drug Related Morbidities

PDRP	Prescription Drug Restriction Program (with AMA)
PDT	Photo-Dynamic Therapy or Product Development Team
PDUFA	Prescription Drug User Fee Act I (1992), II (1997), III (2002), and IV (2007)
PDZ motif	Protein–protein interaction domain (receptor/target)
PE	PharmacoEconomics or PharmacoEpidemiology or Physical Exam or Process Engineering or Pediatric Exclusivity or Pulmonary Embolism or Paclitaxel, Estramustine (CA CT GU or SCLC) or Physical Exercise
PE ratio	Profits to Earnings ratio or Price to Earnings ratio
PEG	PEGylation or PolyEthylene Glycol
PEI	Paul Ehrlich Institute (German regulatory authority)
PERRLA	Pupils Equal Round and Reactive to Light and Accommodation
PET	Positron Emission Tomography
PFK	PhosphoFructoKinase (receptor/target)
PFS	Progression Free Survival
PFT	Pulmonary Function Test
PG	PharmacoGenomics or PharmacoGenetics or Procter & Gamble (company) or PicoGram or ProstaGlandins (-E, -D, or -F) (receptor/target) or Para Gravida (pregnancies)
PGDE	Pharmacologically Guided Dose Escalation
PGE	ProstaGlandin E (receptor/target)
PGI	Prostacyclin (receptor/target)
PGP	P-GlycoProtein (receptor/target)
PGRN	PharmacoGenetics Research Network
PGX	PharmacoGenetics
pH	Hydrogen concentration measurement (acidity of a solution)
PH	Past History
PHA	Public Health Assessment (in HHS)
PHARM Act	PHarmacists Access and Recognition in Medicare Act

PHRP	Partnership for Human Research Protection
PHC	PHarmaCeutics
PHE	PHEnylalanine
PHI	Public Health Insurance or Private Health Insurance
PhRMA	Pharmaceutical Research and Manufacturers Association
PHS	Public Health Service
PI	Package Insert or Principal Investigator or Protease Inhibitor (receptor/target) or Private Investigator
PID	Pelvic Inflammatory Disease
PI-3K	Phosphatidyl Inositol 3-Kinase p110gamma (receptor/target)
PIM	Product Information Management (EMEA requirement for labeling system, based on XML computer language)
PIN	Prostate Intraepithelial Neoplasia or Personal Identification Number
PIP	Pediatric Investigational Plan (FDA requirement) or Phosphatidyl Inositol triPhosphate (receptor/target)
PIPE	Private Investment in Public Equity
PK	PharmacoKinetics or Protein Kinases (receptor/target) or Plasma Kallikrein (receptor/target) or Pyruvate Kinase (receptor/target)
PI3K	Phosphatidyl Inositol-3 Kinase
PKA	Protein Kinase A (receptor/target)
pKa	Acidity of a compound
PKC	Protein Kinase C (receptor/target)
PKS	PolyKetide Synthase (receptor/target)
PL	Pancreatic Lipase (receptor/target) or Product Labeling
P&L	Profits and Loss
PLA	Product License Application or PhosphoLipase A-2 (receptor/target) or Patent License Agreement (with NIH)
PLB	PhosphoLamBan (receptor/target) or PLaceBo
PLC	PhosphoLipase C (receptor/target) or Public Licensed Company (in United Kingdom)

PLGF	PLacental Growth Factor
PM	Project Management or Portfolio Management or Prime Minister or time after 12:00 noon until 11:59 PM or Post Mortem or Poor Metabolizer or Pulmonary Medicine
PMA	PreMarket Approval (for devices)
PMC	Post-Marketing Commitments (to FDA for phase 4 trials or PMS)
PMDA	Pharmaceuticals and Medical Devices Agency (in Japan)
PML	PolyMorphonuclear Leukocyte
PMN	PolyMorphoNuclear leukocyte (WBC)
PMPM	Per Member Per Month
PMS	Post-Marketing Surveillance (for adverse event documentation) or PreMenstrual Syndrome or Post Menopausal Syndrome
PN	Progress Note or Parenteral Nutrition
PNP	Purine Nucleoside Phosphorylase (receptor/target)
PNS	Peripheral Nervous System
PO	Per Os (Latin for oral administration) or Purchase Order or Police Officer
POA	Plan Of Action or Property Owners Association
POC	Point-Of-Care or Post-Operative Care or Proof-Of-Concept or Prednisone, Oncovin, CCNU (CA CT Brain)
POG	Pediatric Oncology Group
POM	Proof Of Mechanism
POMS	Profile Of Mood Scale
POP	Proof Of Principle
POS	Point Of Service or Probability Of Success
PP	Product Portfolio or Product Plans or Public Policy or Project Planning or Post Prandial (Latin for after meals) or Private Patient or PostPartum (after birth) or Plasma Proteins or Publication Plan
PPA	Pharmaceutical Pricing Agreement
PPAR	Peroxisome Proliferator-Activated Receptor (alpha and beta) (receptor/target) or Platelet Protease-Activated Receptor (receptor/target)

PPB	Plasma Protein Binding or Parts Per Billion
PPD	Purified Protein Derivative or Packs Per Day
PPI	Patient Package Insert or Producer Price Index or Proton Pump Inhibitor (receptor/target) or PeptidylPropyl Isomerase (receptor/target)
PPM	Per Patient per Month or Portfolio Planning Management or Parts Per Million
PPO	Preferred Provider Organization
PPQ	Patient Pain Questionnaire
PPP	Public Private Partnerships
PPPM	Prescriptions per Patient Per Month
PPRU	Pediatric Pharmacology Research Unit
PPS	Prospective Payment System (for Medicare drugs)
PPSR	Proposed Pediatric Study Request (to FDA)
PPT	PhosphoenolPyruvate Transferase (receptor/target)
PQ	Performance Qualification
PQA	Pharmacy Quality Alliance (CMS group)
PR	Public Relations or Patient Recruiting or the P to R interval for heart function for atrial activity on ECG or Progesterone Receptor (receptor/target) or Per Rectum or Pulse Rate or Partial Response
PRA	Plasma Renin Activity or Prostanoid Receptor Agonist (receptor/target) or Prostamide Receptor Agonist (receptor/target)
PRBC	Packed Red Blood Cells
PRC	Protocol Review Committee or Peoples Republic of China
PREA	Pediatric Research Equity Act (2003)
PRICE	Pinpoint, Record, Involve, Coach, Evaluate (performance management model by Goldsmith)
PRL	PRoLactin (hormone) (receptor/target)
PRN	Pro Re Nata (Latin for as needed in prescription labels) or Practice Research Networks (in ACCP)
PRO	Patient Reported Outcomes or PROline
PROG	PROGesterone (receptor/target)
ProMACE	Prednisone, Methotrexate, leucovorin, Adriamycin, Cyclophosphamide, Etoposide (CA TX NHL)

PRP	Potentially Responsible Party (with EPA)
PRS	Pain Rating Scale
PS	Professional Services or Post Script or Plastic Surgery or Performance Status
PSA	Prostate Specific Antigen (receptor/target)
PSI	Pounds per Square Inch
PSMA	Prostate Specific Membrane Antigen (receptor/target)
PSR	Professional Sales Representative or Performance Status Review
PST	Pacific Standard Time (United States)
PSUR	Periodic Safety Update Report (for FDA or EMEA)
P&T	Pharmacy and Therapeutics committee
PT	Part-Time or PharmacoTherapy or Physical Therapy or Prothrombin Time or Pharmacology and Toxicology or PinT
PTA	Patent Term Adjustment or Prior To Admission Potassium Transporter ATPase (receptor/target)
PTCA	Percutaneous Transluminal Coronary Angioplasty
PTP	Protein Tyrosine Phosphatase (receptor/target) or PhosphoTyrosine Phosphatase (receptor/target)
PTE	Patent Term Extension
PTEN	Phosphatase and Tensin homologue (receptor/target)
PTK	Protein Tyrosine Kinase (receptor/target)
PTL	Project Team Leader or Program Team Leader
PTM	Post-Translational Modification
PTP	Protein Tyrosine Phosphatase (receptor/target)
PTSD	Post-Traumatic Stress Disorder
PTT	Partial Thromboplastin Time
PTO	Patent and Trademark Office (in United States)
PTVM	PlaTinol, VuMon (CA CT Neuroblastoma)
PUD	Peptic Ulcer Disease
PUMA	Pediatric Use Marketing Authorization (in Europe)
PV	PharmacoVigilance or Process Validation or Present Value
PVA	Prednisone, Vincristine, Asparaginase (CA CT ALL)
PVB	Platinol, Vinblastine, Bleomycin (CA CT Testicular)

PVC	PolyVinyl Chloride or Premature Ventricular Contraction
PVD	Peripheral Vascular Disease
PVDA	Prednisone, Vincristine, Daunorubicin, Asparaginase (CA CT ALL)
PVG	PharmacoViGilance (for adverse event reporting)
PVP	PharmacoVigilance Plan
PWG	Protocol Working Group
PX	Prevention or Pharmacogenetics
PYK	Proline tYrosine Kinase 2 (receptor/target)
PZ	Peripheral Zone
Q	Quarter or every
QA	Quality Assurance or Questions and Answers
QALY	Quality Adjusted Life-Year
QARC	Quality Assurance Review Committee (in NCI groups)
QBR	California institute for Quantitative Biomedical Research
QC	Quality Control
QD	Quid Die (Latin for daily; once per day treatment)
QH	Quid Hora (Latin for every hour)
QID	Quid In Die (Latin for four times a day treatment)
QIO	Quality Improvement Organizations (related to Medicare, part D)
QLI	Quality of Life Index
QLQ	Quality of Life Questionnaire (from EORTC)
QLS	Quality of Life Scale
QOD	Quaque altera Die (Latin for every other day treatment)
QOH	Latin for every Other Hour
QOL	Quality of Life
QP	Qualified Plan
QPQ	Quid Pro Quo (Giving something of value in return for a service or product rendered)
QS	Quantity Sufficient
QSAR	Quantitative Structure Activity Relationship

QT	Quick Time (Something done abruptly) or the Q to T interval in the heart rhythm on an EKG or QuarT
QTC	Quantitative Total Concentration
Q-TWiST	Quality adjusted Time WIthout Symptoms and Toxicity
QW	weekly (drug administration)
QWB	Quality of Well-Being scale
QWBA	Quantitative Whole Body Autoradiography
R	Right or Regular or Roentgen or Revolution
®	Registered name for a product
r^2	coefficient of determination (in statistics, amount of variation)
RA	Regulatory Affairs or Regulatory Authorities or Rheumatoid Arthritis or Retinoic Acid or Risk Assessment
RAC	Recombinant (DNA) Advisory Committee
RAF	gene mutation in tyrosine kinase system (receptor/target)
RAG	Recombinant Activating Gene (receptor/target)
RAID	Rapid Access to Intervention Development (in NCI)
RAM	Regional Area Manager (sales)
RAMP	Receptor Activity Modifying Protein (receptor/target)
R*A*N*D	Rapid Access to NCI Discovery resources
RANTES	Regulated on Activation, Normal T-cell Expressed and Secreted (receptor/target)
RAP	Royal Academy of Physicians (in United Kingdom)
RAPID	Rapid Access to Preventive Intervention Development (in NIH)
RAPS	Regulatory Affairs Professional Society
RAPTOR	Regulatory Associated Protein of mTOR (receptor/target)
RAR	Retinoic Acid Receptor (-alpha, -beta, or -gamma) (receptor/target)
RAS	gene mutation in tyrosine kinase pathway (receptor/target) or Renin-Angiotensin System (receptor/target)

RBC	Red Blood Cell
RBRVS	Resource-Based Relative Value Scale (for payments for healthcare)
R/B ratio	Risk to Benefit ratio (for drugs as assessed by FDA)
RBZ	RiBoZyme (receptor/target)
RCA	Root Cause Analysis
RCC	Renal Cell Carcinoma
RCGP	Royal College of General Practitioners (in United Kingdom)
RCS	Royal College of Surgeons (in United Kingdom)
RCT	Randomized Controlled Trials
RD	Regional Director
R&D	Research and Development
R&D cycle	four stages of research and review for drugs: discovery, pre-clinical, clinical research, and FDA review
RDA	Recommended Daily Allowance
RDC	Remote Data Capture
RDI	Relative Dose Intensity
RECIST	Response Evaluation Criteria In Solid Tumors
RELT	Receptor Expressed in Lymphoid Tissue (receptor/target)
REM	Rapid Eye Movement
REMS	Risk Evaluation Mitigation Strategy
RF	Renal Failure or Renal Function or Respiratory Function or Rheumatoid Factor
RFA	Request For Applications
RfD	ReFerence Dose (in EPA)
RFID	Radio Frequency IDentification (packaging system for a product allowing tracking)
RFLP	Restriction Fragment Length Polymorphism
RFP	Request for Proposals
RGP	Returned Goods Policy
r-H	Recombinant Human
RH	Relative Humidity
RHOA	Ras Homologue gene family member A (receptor/target)

RhF	Rheumatoid Factor
RIA	RadioImmunoAssay
RIR-CaC	Ryanodine-Inositol 1, 4, 5-triphosphate Ca Channel family (receptor/target)
RISC	RNA-Induced Silencing Complex (receptor/target)
RL	Ringer's Lactate or Rhodopsin-Like (receptor/target)
RLD	Reference Listed Drug (with FDA)
RLS	Rate Limiting Step
RM	Regional Manager (in sales) or Risk Management (regarding adverse drug reactions or decision processes) or Regenerative Medicine
RMD	Regional Marketing Director
RMP	Risk Management Program or Risk Management Plan or Reference Medicinal Product (with EMEA)
RN	Registered Nurse
RNA	RiboNucleic Acid
RNR	RiboNucleoside Reductase (receptor/target)
RO	Rule Out or Radiation Oncology
RO1	basic Research grant at NIH
RO3	small Research grant at NIH
ROA	Return On Assets or Route Of Administration
ROCE	Return On Capital Employed
ROCK	Rho Kinases (receptor/target)
ROI	Return On Investment
ROIC	Return On Invested Capital
ROS	Reactive Oxygen Species (receptor/target) or Review Of Systems
ROV	Real Option Value
ROW	Rest Of World
RPA	Renal Physicians Association
RPH	Registered PHarmacist
RR	Recovery Room or Respiratory Rate or Relative Risk or Rest and Relaxation or Response Rate or Ryanodine Receptor (receptor/target) or Recurrence Rate
RRR	Relative Risk Reduction

rRNA	Ribosomal Ribose Nucleic Acid
RS	Ringer's Solution
RSD	Regional Sales Director
RSM	Regional Science Manager or Royal Society of Medicine (in United Kingdom) or Regional Sales Manager
RSS	Review Standards Staff (in FDA)
RT	Randomized Trial or Radiation Therapy or Reverse Transcriptase (receptor/target) or Regional Trainer or RighT or Respiratory Therapist
RTF	Refuse To File (FDA refuses to file NDA due to a deficiency)
RTK	Receptor Tyrosine Kinase (receptor/target)
RTOG	Radiation Therapy Oncology Group
RTPCR	Reverse Transcriptase Polymerase Chain Reaction (receptor/target)
RU	Reviewable Unit (of an NDA through CMA with FDA)
RUC	Resource Utilization Committee (of AMA for Medicare programs)
RV	Residual Volume (in tumors)
Rx	Prescription or Pharmacist or a therapy
RXN	ReactioN
RyR2	Ryanodine Receptor-2 (receptor/target)
S	Single or Sex or Second or Subjective or Standard (review classification of FDA for NDA) or South
S rating	Standard review rating for NDA by FDA
SA	Sustained Action or Surface Area or Sino-Atrial
S-A	Sanofi-Aventis company or Spanish-American
SAB	Scientific Advisory Board
SADS	Schedule for Affective Disorders and Schizophrenia
SAE	Serious Adverse Event
SAF	Standard Analytical Files (data from Medicare)
SAFE	Secure Access For Everyone (FDA initiative with industry)
SAG	Scientific Advisory Groups (in Europe for EMEA)
SAGE	Serial Analysis of Gene Expression

SAL	Scientific Affairs Liaison
SAM	Selective Adhesion Molecule inhibitors (receptor/ target) or S-AdenosylMethionine synthetase (receptor/ target) or Sales Area Manager
SAR	Structure Activity Relationship or Steroid 5-Alpha-Reductase (receptor/target)
SBD	Structure Based Design
SBE	Subacute Bacterial Endocarditis
SBIR	Small Business Incentive Research (grant or loan from U.S. government)
SBL	Small Business Loan
SBMP	Similar Biological Medicinal Product (in Europe, EMEA)
SBOA	Summary Basis Of Approval (from FDA for an NDA)
SBP	Systolic Blood Pressure
SC	SubCutaneous or South Carolina or Southern California or SubClavian or Spinal Cord or Supportive Care
SCF	Stem Cell Factor (receptor/target)
SCGF	Stem Cell Growth Factor (receptor/target)
SCID	Structured Clinical Interview for DSM-4 or Severe Compromised Immune Deficiency
SCLC	Small Cell Lung Cancer
SCCM	Society for Critical Care Medicine
SCR	Serum CReatinine
SCT	Single Controlled Trial
SD	Stable Disease or Standard Deviation or South Dakota or Streptozocin, Doxorubicin (CA TX Pancreas) or Steroid Dehydrogenase (receptor/target) or Sales Director
SDB	Safety DataBase
SDS	Self-rating Depression Scale (by Zung)
SDTM	Study Data Tabulation Model
S&M	Sales and Marketing
SE	Side Effect or Surrogate Endpoint or Standard Error
SEC	SECretin (receptor/target) or Security and Exchange Commission

SEER	Surveillance, Epidemiology, and End Results (database of Medicare)
SELEX	Systematic Evolution of Ligands by Exponential Enrichment
SEM	Standard Error of the Mean or Scanning Electron Microscope
SEP	Self-Employed retirement Plan
SER	SERine
SERM	Selective Estrogen Receptor Modulator (receptor/target)
SF	Salt Free or Sugar Free or Spinal Fluid or Synovial Fluid
SF-36	Short Form (Questionnaire of 36 questions to assess general psychiatric and health well being of patients in many disease areas)
SFAS	Statement of Financial Accounting Standards (in company reports)
SFDA	State Food and Drug Administration (in China)
SG	Specific Gravity
SG&A	Selling, General, and Administrative (costs of operations)
S&H	Shipping and Handling
SHARE	Submission Harmony And Reliable E-business (in FDA)
SHM	Society of Hospital Medicine
SHIP	SH2 InositolPhosphatase (receptor/target)
SHP	Src Homology Phosphatase 2 (receptor/target)
SHX	Social History
SI	Sub-Investigator or Small Intestine or prefix for International system of measures, preceding a unit of measure)
SIAC	Special Interest Area Community (of DIA)
SIADH	Syndrome of Inappropriate AntiDiuretic Hormone
SICU	Surgical Intensive Care Unit
SINQ	S (SEER) INQuiry system
SIP	Sickness Impact Profile
siRNA	Short Interfering RiboNucleic Acid (receptor/target)
SKU	Sales Configuration Unit or Shelf Keeping Unit

SL	SubLingual
SLA	Service Licensing Agreement or Simple Letter of Agreement (with NIH)
SLE	Systemic Lupus Erythematosus
SLP	Src-homology-2 domain containing Leukocyte Protein (receptor/target)
SMART	Specific, Measurable, Accurate, Reasonable, and Timely (for Objectives)
SMBG	Self-Monitored Blood Glucose
SMD	Small Molecule Drug
SMDA	Safe Medical Devices Act (1990)
SME	Small and Medium-sized Enterprises (office in EMEA)
SMF	Streptozocin, Mitomycin-C, Fluorouracil (CA CT Pancreas)
SMO	Site Management Organization (clinical research) or Sales Management Organization
SMZ	SulfaMethoxaZole
SN	SigNs (of disease in a patient) or SiNgle
SNAP	SyNaptosomal Associated Protein (receptor/target)
SNDA	Supplemental New Drug Application
SNF	Skilled Nursing Facility
SNM	Society of Nuclear Medicine
SNOMED	Systematized NOmenclature of MEDicine (FDA PI language)
SNP	Single Nucleotide Polymorphism
SNS	Society of Neurology Surgeons or Sympathetic Nervous System
SO	Safety Officer or Strike Out or Surgical Oncology
SOAP	Symptoms, Objective findings, Assessment, and Plan (for medical chart notes)
SOB	Shortness Of Breath
SOC	Suppressor Of Cytokine signaling (receptor/target) or Standard Of Care
SOD	SuperOxide Dismutase (receptor/target)
SOP	Standard Operating Procedure or Stock Option Program

S1P	Sphingosine 1 Phosphate (receptor/target)
SOX	Sarbanes OXley Act (information privacy and business practices) (2002)
SP	SPecies or Signal Peptidase (receptor/target) or Serine Proteases (receptor/target) or Status Post (after)
S-P	Schering-Plough company
S&P 500	Standards & Poors 500 (companies in a stock exchange)
SPA	Special Protocol Assessment (with FDA)
SPAP	State Pharmaceutical Assistance Programs
SPC	Supplementary Patent (Protection) Certificate (in Europe) or Sodium Potassium Chloride cotransporter (receptor/target)
SP GR	SPecific GRavity
SPL	Structured Product Labeling (FDA requirement for NDA Labeling, using XML system)
SPM	Strategic Project (or Program) Management
SQ	Subcutaneous or SQuare
SQL	Structured Query Language
SR	Sustained Release or Statistical Report or Steroid 5-alpha-Reductase (receptor/target)
SRIF	Somatostatin Release Inhibiting Factors (receptor/target)
SRS-A	Slow Reactive Substance of Anaphylaxis
SS	Social Security or Saline Solution or Social Services or Sample Size
S/S	Signs and Symptoms
SSA	Social Security Administration or Act
SSAD	Succinate SemiAldehyde Dehydrogenase (receptor/target)
SSDI	Social Security Disability Income
SSN	Social Security Number
SSRI	Serotonin Selective Reuptake Inhibitor (receptor/target)
ST	STem Cell or Stress Test or Skin Test
STAT	Signal Transducer and Activator of Transcription (-1 up to -6) (receptor/target) or STATim (Latin for immediately)

STD	Sexually Transmitted Disease or Severely Toxic Dose (in rodents)
STDM	Standard Tabulation Data Model (part of CDISC)
STF	Study Tagging Files
STMT	STateMenT
STR	Structure Toxicity Relationship
STS	Society of Thoracic Surgeons
STTR	Small business Technology Transfer Research grants
SUPAC	Scale-Up and Post-Approval Changes (after NDA for FDA review)
SUR	SulphonylUrea (-1, -2) Receptor (receptor/target)
SUV	Small Unilamellar Vesicle
SVAT	Serotonin Vesicular Amine Transporter (receptor/target)
SVC	SerViCe
SVP	Senior Vice-President or Small Volume Parenterals
SVT	SupraVentricular Tachycardia
SW	SWeden or SWitzerland or Social Worker
SWF	Single White Female
SWFI	Sterile Water For Injection
SWOG	SouthWest Oncology Group
SWOT	Strength, Weakness, Opportunity, and Threat analysis
SWX	SWiss stock eXchange
SYK	Spleen tYrosine Kinase (receptor/target)
SX	Surgery or Symptoms or SeX
T	Time or Temperature or Tablespoon or Treated or Teaspoon
T2	Dactinomycin, Doxorubicin–Doxorubicin, Oncovin, Cyclophosphamide–Oncovin, Cyclophosphamide–Oncovin, Cyclophosphamide (CA CT cycles Sarcoma)
TA	Therapeutic Area or Teaching Assistant or Transporter ATPase (receptor/target) or Tentative Approval (of NDA by FDA)
T ½	Half-life of the concentration of a drug or chemical usually in blood

TAA	Tumor-Associated Antigen
TAB	TABlet
TACE	TNF-Alpha-Converting Enzyme (receptor/target)
TACI	Transmembrane Activator and CAML-Interactor (receptor/target)
TAP	Technical Assistance Program (in NIH)
TB	TuBerculosis or Tubulin Beta chain (receptor/target)
TBA	To Be Added or To Be Announced
TBD	To Be Determined
TBI	Total Body Irradiation
TBL	TaBLespoon
TBW	Total Body Water or Total Body Weight
TC	Thioguanine, Cytarabine (CA CT ANLL) or Tissue Culture or Troponin C (receptor/target)
TCA	TriCyclic Antidepressant
TCM	Traditional Chinese Medicine
TCR	T-Cell Receptors (receptor/target)
TD	TransDermal (administration) or Target Discovery or Tardive Dyskinesia or Thyroxine 5-Deiodinase (receptor/target)
TDM	Therapeutic Drug Monitoring
TE	Trial Endpoints or Tissue Engineering
T&E	Travel and Entertainment (expenses) or Time and Events
TEFRA	Tax Equity and Fiscal Responsibility Act
TF	Tissue Factor (receptor/target) or Transcription Factor (receptor/target)
TFPI	Tissue Factor Pathway Inhibitor (receptor/target)
TELECOM	TELEphone COMmunications
TGA	Therapeutic Goods Administration (in Australia)
TGF	Transforming Growth Factor (receptor/target)
TH	Thyroid Hormone (receptor/target) or Tyrosine 3-Hydroxylase (receptor/target)
T_H1	T-1-Helper cell (lymphocyte) (receptor/target)
T_H2	T-2-Helper cell (lymphocyte) (receptor/target)

THA	Total Hip Arthroplasty
THC	TetraHydroCannabinol (receptor/target)
THR	THRombin (receptor/target) or THReonine or Thyroid Hormone Receptor (receptor/target)
TI	Therapeutic Index or TopoIsomerase (receptor/target)
TIA	Transient Ischemic Attack
TID	Tres In Die (Latin for three times a day treatment)
TIM	TopoIsoMerase (receptor/target)
TIMP	Tissue Inhibitor of MetalloProteinase (receptor/target)
TIV	Trivalent Influenza Vaccines
TIW	Three times a Week
TK	Tyrosine Kinase (receptor/target) or Tissue Kallikrein (receptor/target)
TKA	Total Knee Arthroplasty
TKI	Tyrosine Kinase Inhibitor (receptor/target)
TKR	Tyrosine Kinase Receptors (receptor/target)
TL	Thought Leader or Team Leader
TLC	Total Lung Capacity or Tender Loving Care or Thin Layer Chromatography
TLO	Technology Licensing Organization
TLR	Toll-Like Receptors (in immune diseases) (receptor/target)
TM	TradeMark (for a product name)
TMA	Tissue MicroArray
Tmax	Time to MAXimum concentration
TMP	TriMethoPrim
TNA	Total Nutrient Admixture
TNF	Tumor Necrosis Factor (-alpha) (receptor/target)
TNM	Tumor (size), Number, and Metastasis (system in staging cancers)
TOC	Table Of Contents (for Toxicology studies in animals)
TOPO	TOPOisomerase (-1 or -2) (receptor/target) or TOPOtecan
TOX	TOXicology
TPA	Tissue Plasminogen Activator (receptor/target)

TPD	Therapeutic Products Directorate (Canadian health agency)
TPK	Tyrosine Protein Kinase (receptor/target)
TPMT	ThioPurine MethylTransferase (receptor/target)
TPO	ThromboPOietin (receptor/target) or Thyroid PerOxidase (receptor/target)
TPOR	ThromboPOietin Receptor (receptor/target)
TPP	Target Product Profile or Therapeutic Product Programme (in Canada) or Thiamine Pyrophosphate (receptor/target)
TR	TReatment or Thioredoxin Reductase (receptor/target) or Testosterone Receptor (receptor/target)
TRAF6	TNF Receptor Associated Factor 6 (receptor/target)
TRAIL	Tumor-necrosis factor Related Apoptosis Inducing Ligand (receptor/target)
TRAMP	TRansgenic Adenocarcinoma of Mouse Prostate (receptor/target)
TRC	The RNAi Consortium (library of RNA and technologies)
TRIM	TcR-Interacting Molecule (receptor/target)
TRIPS	Trade-Related aspects of Intellectual Property rightS (with WTO)
TRP	TRyPtophan
TRP-CC	Transient Receptor Potential Calcium Channel (receptor/target)
TRPV	Transient Receptor Potential Vanilloid (receptor/target)
TS	Thymidylate Synthase (receptor/target)
TSA	Tumor Specific Antigen or Transportation Security Administration
TSC	Thiazide-sensitive Sodium Chloride cotransporter (receptor/target)
TSH	Thyroid Stimulating Hormone (receptor/target)
TSP	TeaSPoon
TT	T-Test (statistical test) or Thrombin Time
TTP	Time To Progression or Time to Tumor Progression
TV	Tumor Volume or TeleVision

TW	Therapeutic Window
TX	Treatment or Therapy or TeXas
TXA	ThromboXane A synthetase (receptor/target)
TXB	ThromboXane B synthetase (receptor/target)
TYK	TYrosine Kinase (receptor/target)
TZ	Transition Zone
TZD	ThiaZolineDiones

U	Unit
UA	Urine Analysis or Uric Acid
UBMTA	Uniform Biological Materials Transfer Agreement (with NIH)
UC	Ulcerative Colitis or Urea Clearance
UCS	Union of Concerned Scientists
UD	Unit Dosing or UniDimensional
UGT	Uridine diphosphate GlucurosylTransferase (receptor/target)
UHC	University Health-systems Consortia
UK	United Kingdom (England, Scotland, Wales, and Northern Ireland) or UnKnown
UL	Underwriters Laboratory
ULN	Under Lower limits of Normal
UN	United Nations (international organization)
UNGI	United Nations Global Impact (corporate responsibility)
UNK	UNKnown
UPS	Ubiquitin-Proteasome System (receptor/target) or United Parcel Service
UR	Utilization Review
URAA	Uruguay Round Agreement Act (1994; for international patents)
URI	Upper Respiratory Infection
US	United States
USAN	United States Approved Name
USDA	United States Department of Agriculture

USP	United States Pharmacopoeia
USPHS	United States Public Health Service
USPS	United State Postal Service
USPTO	United States Patent and Trademark Office
USRDS	United States Registry of Disease Statistics
UT	UroTensin (receptor/target) or University of Texas
UTD	Up To Date
UTI	Urinary Tract Infection
UTSA	Uniform Trade Secrets Act (United States)
UVA	UltraViolet light A band
UVB	UltraViolet light B band
UV	UltraViolet radiation
V	Value or Variance or Volume or Velocity or Voltage or Virus or Vein or Vitamin or five in Latin or Vomit or Variable
VA	Veterans Administration or Visual Acuity
VAC	Vincristine, Adriamycin, Cyclophosphamide (CA CT–SCLC, Germ cell) or Vincristine, dactinomycin, Cyclophosphamide (CA CT Sarcoma)
VAD	Vincristine, Adriamycin, Dexamethasone (CA CT MM or Wilms)
VAI	Voluntary Action Indicated (FDA letter asking for compliance)
VAL	VALine
VAMP	Vesicle-Associated Membrane Protein (receptor/target)
VAN	VANilloid receptor (receptor/target)
VAP	Vincristine, Asparaginase, Prednisone (CA CT ALL)
VAS	Visual Analogue Scale
VASC	Vacuolar ATP Synthase Catalytic subunit A (receptor/target)
VASO	VASOpressin (receptor/target)
VATH	Vinblastine, Adriamycin, THiotepa (CA CT Breast)
VB	VinBlastine, methotrexate (CA CT GU)
VBAP	Vincristine, BCNU, Adriamycin, Prednisone (CA CT MM)

VBC	Vinblastine, Bleomycin, Cisplatin (CA CT MM)
VBMCP	Vincristine, BCNU, Melphalan, Cyclophosphamide, Prednisone (CA CT MM)
VBP	Vinblastine, Bleomycin, Platinol (CA CT GU)
VC	Venture Capital (for investment in a company) or Vepesid, Carboplatin (CA CT SCLC)
VCAM	Vascular Cell-Adhesion Molecule (receptor/target)
VCAP	Vincristine, Cyclophosphamide, Adriamycin, Prednisone (CA CT MM)
VD	Volume of Distribution or Venereal Disease
VDP	Vinblastine, Dacarbazine, Platinol (CA CT MM)
VDR	Vitamin D Receptor (receptor/target)
VEGF	Vascular Endothelial Growth Factor -1, -2 (receptor/target)
VF	Ventricular Fibrillation
VHA	Volunteer Hospitals Association of America or Veterans Health Administration
VIP	Vasoactive Intestinal Peptide (receptor/target) or Vinblastine Iphosphamide, Platinol (CA CT Testicular or SCLC)
VITD3	VITamin D-3 (receptor/target)
VRER	Vitamin K Epoxide Reductase (receptor/target)
VLA	Very Late Antigen (receptor/target)
VLDL	Very Low Density Lipoprotein
VLP	Virus-Like Particle
VOC	Volatile Organic Compounds (in Europe, environmental impact requirement)
VOL	VOLume or VOLuntary
VP	Vice-President
VPP	Voltage-gated Potassium channel (receptor/target)
VPR	VasoPressin (-1A, -1B, -2) Receptor
VR	Vasopressin (-1A, -1B, -2) Receptor
VRE	Vancomycin Resistant Enterococcus
VS	Vital Signs or VerSus
VSC	Voltage-gated Sodium Channel (receptor/target)
Vss	Volume of distribution at Steady State

VT	Ventricular Tachycardia
VTE	Venous ThromboEmbolism
V:V	Volume to Volume ratio
W	White or Women or With or Wife or Water or West
WAC	Wholesale Acquisition Cost
WACC	Weighted Average Cost of Capital
WAIS	Wechsler Adult Intelligence Scale
WASP	White Anglo-Saxon Male
WB	Whole Blood
WBC	White Blood Cell
WBRT	Whole Brain Radiation Therapy
WFI	Water For Injection
WHI	Women's Health Initiative
WHO	World Health Organization
WIC	Women, Infants and Children (CMS program)
WIPO	World Intellectual Property Organization
WK	WeeK or WorK
WL	Warning Letter (from the FDA DDMAC)
WLF	Washington Legal Foundation
WMA	World Medical Association
WNL	Within Normal Limits
WR	Written Request (from FDA to perform pediatric study)
WT	WeighT
WTO	World Trade Organization
WTP	Willing-To-Pay (type of pharmacoeconomic study) or Willingness To Participate
W:V	Weight to Volume ratio
WW	World Wide or Weight to Weight ratio
WWW	World Wide Web
X	average (in statistics) or ten (Roman numeral) or times
X^2	chi-squared (statistical test)
XD	Xanthine Dehydrogenase (receptor/target)

XIAP	X-Linked Inhibitor of APoptosis (receptor/target)
XL	eXtended reLease (Formulation) or eXtra Luxury or forty (Roman numeral) or eXtra Large
XML	eXtensible Markup Language
XO	Cross-Over (in study design) or Cross-Out
XR	eXtended Release or X-Ray
XT	eXtended Time
XX	twenty (Roman numeral)
Y-90	Yttrium-90 (radioactive nuclide in drugs)
YD	YarD
YO	Years Old
YR	YeaR
Y-site	intravenous administration of two drugs using two lines that come together to form a Y
YTD	Year To Date
Zs	sleep

TERMS AND PHRASES OF THE BIOPHARMA LANGUAGE

A

Abbreviated New Drug Application (ANDA): An application to the FDA for marketing approval for a generic version of a marketed product. The application includes conditions of use, active ingredients, route of administration, dosage form and strength, bioequivalence, labeling, chemistry, manufacturing and controls, samples, patent certification, and financial certification or disclosure.

Absorption: The property of a product that involves its passage from its formulation across biologic membranes into the bloodstream at its site of administration. Factors that impact the absorption of a product include its solubility and permeability, the effect of transporters (e.g., PGP, OATP), in vitro in vivo correlation, absolute/relative bioavailability and bioequivalence, and effects of concurrently consumed substances (excipients, food, beverages).

Accelerated approval: FDA approval in a shorter timeframe for new drugs that possibly can provide meaningful therapeutic benefit over existing treatments for serious or life-threatening illnesses. The accelerated timeframe often necessitates use of a surrogate endpoint to demonstrate efficacy. The labeling will contain restricted use provisions. This status solely is designated by the FDA.

ACR (American College of Rheumatology) Scores: In the assessment of rheumatoid arthritis and related inflammatory joint diseases, a composite scoring system set-up by the ACR assesses number of painful and swollen joints and employs three levels of improvement in each patient in the signs and symptoms at 20%, 50%, and 70%, as ascertained by the assessing health-care professional.

Action letter: A letter from the FDA to a sponsor regarding their application for marketing authorization (approval, non-approval, or approvable). An action letter is a letter to an applicant that is issued after the complete review of a filed application. If the letter is not an approval letter, then it will set forth in detail the specific deficiencies and, where appropriate, the actions necessary to place the application in condition for approval. An action letter may contain additional or fewer deficiencies than were provided in previously issued drug regulatory letters, depending on the final review of the application and supervisory evaluation by Division and/or Office Directors. The issuance of an action letter completes the review cycle for a pending application. It is the benchmark by which the agency's performance against the PDUFA application review goals is measured.

Action plans: The specific activities in a marketing plan performed by the sales staff or others for the sales and marketing promotion of a product, as well as medical education, including materials to be used, timeframe for completion, and persons responsible.

Active pharmaceutical ingredient (API): The compound(s) in a product that are responsible for its desired actions. The description requires elucidation of structure, that is, stereochemistry, isomers, polymorphs, and salt selection, secondary and tertiary structure, glycosylation, and biological activity.

Active control: In a clinical study, a pharmacologically active and documented useful compound for a disease being given to a comparison group versus a group receiving the product being studied.

Activities of daily living (ADL): The activities a person performs for normal daily life, such as feeding or bathing, cleaning the house, and shopping.

Adaptive trials: Clinical studies that prospectively build into the design changes in patient allocation to treatment groups while patients are still being recruited at predetermined points, based on interim responses during the study. This allows researchers to improve expected patient outcomes during the experiment while still being able to reach good statistical decisions in a timely fashion. One form of adaptive trial design allows a scientifically predetermined outcome to be measured and allows randomization to be allocated proportionally toward patient populations that are enriched by the characteristics that are likely to predict a positive outcome. For example, this might involve a type of tumor or a specific tumor marker in the case of cancer trials.

Addressable population: Group of patients that have the target disease in question (characterized by, for example, age, sex, disease severity and duration, prior therapy) and may potentially be amenable to treatment with the target product being studied or marketed.

Adequate and well-controlled study (AWCS): In order to detect real changes produced by a drug in a study and not bias or placebo effects, the following eight characteristics apply to all AWCS studies in an application for marketing authorization (NDA/BLA) to the FDA: (1) a clear statement of objectives, (2) a precise design permitting valid comparison to an appropriately set up control group with quantitative assessments (placebo, concurrent dose, no treatment concurrent, active treatment concurrent, or historical), (3) patient selection demonstrating disease in patients, (4) patient assignment avoiding bias and assuring comparability, (5) bias minimized, (6) patient assessments reliable, well-defined, and without bias, (7) methods of analysis detailed, and (8) analysis of results adequate for drug effects with description of methods.

Ad hoc letters: Product letters written de novo by a sponsor/manufacturer for new medical information questions posed usually by healthcare professionals to the manufacturer of a product.

Adverse event (AE): Any reaction in a patient to a drug or biological product given at normal doses that negatively impacts health. An adverse event may occur in a clinical study or spontaneous report during normal clinical use. They also can be defined as events associated with use of drug in humans, whether or not they are considered drug related, that are undesired and potentially harmful to a patient.

Adverse Event Reporting System (AERS): A computerized information database designed to support the FDA's post-marketing safety surveillance program for all approved drug and therapeutic biologic products. Adverse events from spontaneous reports are entered in the database. The ultimate goal of the AERS is to improve the public health by providing the best available tools for storing and analyzing safety reports.

Advertising: Promotional materials of a product produced by a company or its agencies intended to sell the product, including all visual materials, for example, printed documents in press (journals, newspapers), printed sales pieces, and consumer ads (television, radio, internet).

Advertising copy: Content and presentation of promotional materials for the purpose of selling a product established by regulations. The materials cannot be false or misleading, and must contain "fair balance" of benefits and risks. Advertising campaigns are submitted for FDA review and clearance. The FDA reacts particularly to efficacy and safety and protection of the public health and welfare.

Advisory committee: To keep up with the challenges that the FDA's full-time experts face when reviewing innovative and rapidly evolving technologies, the agency hires "special government employees," whose opinions complement its goals to provide safe and effective products. These outside advisers make up the FDA's technical and scientific advisory committees. The primary role of an advisory committee is to provide independent advice that will contribute to the quality of the agency's regulatory decision-making and lend credibility to the product review process. Although advisory committees have a prominent role in the product approval stage, they are sometimes included earlier in the product development cycle and are asked to consider issues relating to products already on the market. Committees typically are asked to comment on whether adequate data support approval, clearance, or licensing of a medical product for marketing. Advisory committees also may recommend that the FDA request additional studies or suggest changes to a product's labeling. Their recommendations are just that—advice—and do not bind the agency to any decision. Although committee discussions and final votes are very important to the FDA, the final regulatory decision rests with the agency. Membership in advisory committees must be "fairly balanced"—that is, as open and inclusive as possible—according to the law. Committee membership is expected to include ethnic, gender, and geographic diversity, as well as people with recognized expertise and judgment in a specific field, such as clinicians and researchers. Most members of the FDA's drug advisory committees, for example, are physician-scientists whose specialties or research involve the kinds of products being reviewed. Other members might include statisticians, epidemiologists, nutritionists, and toxicologists (experts in preclinical [animal] studies). The FDA also insists on getting industry and public perspectives, and nearly all committees include industry and consumer representation.

Advisory committee meetings: Public meetings of experts for the therapeutic area of a product that are sponsored by divisions within CDER and CBER to provide medical and pharmaceutical advice.

Advocacy group: A group of people from the public at large in a specific medical arena that represent a disease and promote its cure and support of the patients, including soliciting funds, educating the public, lobbying efforts, and sponsoring research.

Age groups: As defined by FDA, Neonate: birth to 1 month; Infant: 1 month to 2 years; Children: 2 to 12 years; Adolescent: 12 to 16 years.

Agency for National Research: Regulatory agency for product approvals and oversight of the pharmaceutical industry in France.

Alert reports: Fifteen-day reports of serious and unexpected adverse reactions with a drug during its research or after marketing to the FDA by the sponsor or applicant of an NDA.

Alliance: A business venture wherein two or more companies or entities work together on a venture for research and development, sales and marketing, and manufacturing or combination of the aforementioned activities.

Allometric scaling: In dosing for pharmacokinetic studies, interspecies scaling of PK data to predict human PK is based on similarities in physiology and anatomy among species. Allometric scaling can be conducted using the following relationship: $CL = Wt^b$, where the total clearance is scaled based on the body weights of various species. Similarly volume of distribution can also be scaled, which is generally proportional to the body weight. Generally, the exponent, b, has a value of 0.75 for clearance and 1 for volume of distribution.

Alternative medicines: Products that are not considered drugs or biological products and are used to treat diseases, for example, vitamins, minerals, and natural products from the environment.

Ambulatory payment classification (APC): Categorization by CMS for reimbursement for drug products given in outpatient settings.

Ampule: A container system for a liquid product that is made of glass and needs to be broken open to access and withdraw the medication.

Analysis of variance (ANOVA): A statistic that is calculated in research or clinical studies that represents the variability of data around an average score for a parameter.

Analyst: (1) A person employed by an investment company who assesses a company for its value to the public. (2) A person at a biopharma company who usually works in market research or information technology assessing data and information.

Analytical assays: Multiple assays are needed to ensure product consistency and potency. Common consistency assays include appearance, concentration, pH, ionic strength, sterility, endotoxin, and purity. Potency assays focus on specific properties of the product, such as, for antibodies, binding, antibody-dependent cell-cytotoxicity, functional inhibition; for enzymes, catalytic activity; for recombinant proteins, functional activity or inhibition; and for drugs, functional activity or inhibition.

Animal toxicology studies: Assessment of a compound's effects in animals to determine a toxic dose and its harmful actions, including acute and chronic dosing studies, tests for assessment of genetic safety, tests for adverse events in reproductive capability, and assessments of hematology, chemistry, renal and liver function, and histology (gross and microscopic) tests.

Annual report: (1) Applicant must submit to the FDA within 60 days of the anniversary of the U.S. approval a summary of significant new information from the previous year that might affect the safety, effectiveness, or labeling of the drug product. Other information included is any actions taken by the applicant because of the new information, distribution information for the product, current labeling being used, any changes in CMC, clinical data (published trials, summary of completed unpublished trials, any pediatric data), status reports of post-marketing study commitments required by the FDA, advertisements and promotional labeling (specimens). (2) Yearly report prepared by publicly traded companies for distribution to shareholders and potential investors. It includes a status of current research projects, an overview of their financials, societal commitments, new major initiatives in research, new hires, and/or manufacturing.

Antisense: A ribonucleotide (RNA) molecule that hybridizes with a complementary RNA molecule that is causing adverse biologic effects and stops RNA function.

Applicant: The entity who submits a marketing application to the FDA or other regulatory authority for approval of a drug, device, or biologic product.

Approvable letter: The document created by the FDA for a sponsor of an NDA or BLA stating their product potentially can be approved, if they will meet certain requirements dictated by the FDA, for example, a follow-up study to be done, or changes in the labeling.

Approval letter: The document created by the FDA for a sponsor of an NDA or BLA stating their product is approved for marketing in the United States based on the efficacy, safety, and product quality established in their application.

Aptamer: Single-stranded RNA or double stranded DNA molecules made up of short lengths of nucleic acids that form 3-dimensional structures and can bind to specific endogenous targets to produce its biologic action.

Area under the concentration curve (AUC): A measure of a product's bioavailability (absorption and drug levels over time) on a graph. It is the physical area below the line in a plot of drug levels (y-axis) versus time (x-axis) with a line representing various drug concentrations in the graph.

Asset: Cash, marketable securities, receivables, property (real or intellectual), inventory, and equipment of a company.

Associated with drug use: A reasonable possibility that the experience may have been caused by the drug, as judged by a health professional submitting a report to FDA.

Audience: A group of people (providers, payers, patients, policymakers, and/or press) or institutions in a geographic region, and/or for a particular disease, and/or within a therapeutic category, targeted by a company for research, a medical education program, or marketing activity.

Audit: Evaluation of a product, system, application, finances, or company by an outside group, often a regulatory agency, including usually a visit to establish compliance with operating procedures or plans. An audit is a formal examination and verification of accounts, processes, or results in the conduct of clinical trials by sponsor and the FDA. Audits of case report forms are common. Audits of safety data are very important to continually monitor the safety of subjects in a trial.

Audit trail: The set and sequence of information (documents, files, reports, etc.) that details the order of events in an audit.

Authorized generic drug: The original manufacturer for a branded drug whose patent will expire in the near future permits the sale of a generic version of their drug by a subsidiary or another agreed upon generic company as a concurrent alternative to existing sales of the branded drug.

Automated call distribution (ACD): Customer service or investor telephone lines incorporate a system that refers telephone calls to prespecified numbers automatically, usually based on the drug name, type of service needed, or contact person.

Average manufacturer's price (AMP): The average price paid to a manufacturer by wholesalers for drugs distributed to retail pharmacies. Average manufacturer's price was a benchmark created by Congress in 1990 in calculating Medicaid rebates and is not publicly available. Federal Supply Schedule prices, as well as prices associated with direct sales to HMOs and hospitals, are excluded from AMP under the rebate program. The Congressional Budget Office estimates AMP to be about 20 percent less than the average wholesale price (defined below) for more than 200 drug products frequently purchased by Medicaid recipients.

Average sales price (ASP): The weighted average of all non-Federal sales to wholesalers and is the net of charge backs, discounts, rebates, and other benefits tied to the purchase of the drug product, whether it is paid to the wholesaler or the retailer.

Average unit price (AUP): The manufacturer's sale price less all required adjustments included in the average manufacturer's price.

Average wholesale price (AWP): A price for a product to wholesalers, averaged across all wholesalers. Drug products are sold by manufacturers with a specific and variable price to wholesalers who distribute the drug product to retail outlets or other end-user customers. Each wholesaler will have an individualized "wholesale" price, based on various factors, such as the volume of business, discounts, or extra services provided.

B

Bacteriostatic water for injection (BWI): Sterile water containing a preservative that retards bacterial growth and is used for the dilution and preparation of drug and biological products for parenteral administration to patients.

Balanced scorecard (in PPM): The assessment for a business area of all the processes, inputs, and outcomes in managing project functionality, quality, and outcomes, in areas such as process excellence, commercial value, sustained innovation, learning and growing, and customer satisfaction.

Batch: A specific lot of manufactured product.

Best Pharmaceuticals for Children Act (BPCA): U.S. legislation in 2002 fostering clinical research in children, including such general elements as expanded marketing exclusivity (6 months) for pediatric labeling, FDA–NIH collaboration being established for research especially on off-patent products, Office of Pediatric Therapeutics in the FDA established, and all adverse events being reported for 1 year following approval. For on-patent products, industry or the FDA initiates a request for pediatric research and labeling, and written requests are to be done by the FDA. For off-patent, specific drugs are designated for research by NIH study.

Best-in-class (BIC): The product approved for use in a specific disease, therapeutic area, or pharmacologic class that is the best based on its highest level of usage (sales) among its competitors, usually because of a product's clinical advantages and the marketing prowess of the manufacturer.

Best practices: A set of activities and their related processes and procedures to perform a function at the highest possible level of competency, often based on published operating guidelines from recognized experts in the field, whether in the government or in private sectors of business.

Best price: The lowest price available from a manufacturer during a rebate period to any wholesaler, retailer, health maintenance organization, non-profit entity, or government entity within the United States. It includes cash discounts, free goods contingent on sales, volume discounts, and rebates. Best price excludes prices to the Indian Health Service (IHS), Department of Veterans Affairs (DVA), Department of Defense (DoD), the Public Health Service (PHS), 340B covered entities, Federal Supply Schedule (FSS) and State pharmaceutical assistance programs, depot prices, and nominal pricing. Best price includes cash discounts, free goods that are contingent upon purchase, volume discounts, and rebates.

Bioavailability (BA): The rate and extent of drug absorption based on blood level measurements over time, usually measured by the area under the concentration curve of a plot of blood levels versus time.

Bioequivalence (BE): Two versions of the same product or drug must deliver the same amount of active ingredient into the patient's bloodstream in the same timeframe. Bioequivalence is usually used for a generic drug compared to a reference standard.

Biogeneric: A biological product that has the same physical, pharmacokinetic, and biologic properties of a patented biological product, manufactured through the same processes (e.g., plasmids, host cells, fermentation, and purification for recombinant proteins) and based on various chemical and biologic analyses; also called a biosimilar.

Bioinformatics: A discipline or system that collects, stores, manipulates, correlates, and analyzes large banks of biological data and information.

Biologics License Application (BLA): The set of forms and documents created by a biotechnology or pharmaceutical company for a biological product that are provided to the FDA to obtain marketing approval. The main content is the compilation and summary of clinical research establishing safety and efficacy, along with manufacturing process and product testing establishing product quality.

Biologicals: Antibodies, blood products, enzymes, hormones, gene therapies, growth factors, oligonucleotides, peptides, proteins (other), cells and tissues, liposomal products, vaccines or analogous products, used in the prevention, mitigation, or cure of a disease.

Biologic product: Any virus, serum, toxin, vaccine, blood, blood component or derivative, allergenic product, or analogous product applicable in prevention, treatment, or cure of disease or injuries. They are a subset of "drug products" distinguished by the biological manufacturing process.

Biologics response advisory committee: An FDA committee of experts for biological products that potentially produce pharmacologic actions in patients. The experts advise, for example, about product approvals, product usage issues, and practice guidelines with the products.

Biologic response modifier (BRM): A biologic product that modifies the activites of normal physiologic processes in the body, for example, interferons, colony stimulating factors, interleukins.

Biomarker: A biologic measurement, for example, the presence or absence of an enzyme, receptor, other protein or peptide, a mutated mRNA, or a genetic mutation, that differentiates patient subpopulations and is indicative of a disease, the disease severity, a stage in a disease, a subpopulation with the disease that are differentiated by their drug response, or a subpopulation of people with a different drug activity or pharmacokinetics. Biomarkers may or may not be relevant for monitoring clinical outcome.

Biometrics: A method of verifying an individual's identity based on measurement of the individual's physical features or repeatable actions that are unique to the individual and are measurable.

Biopharmaceutical: Term also used usually as an alternative to biological.

Biopharmaceutics Classification System (BCS): Goals of the BCS are (1) To improve the efficiency of drug development and the review process by recommending a strategy for identifying expendable clinical bioequivalence tests. (2) To recommend a class of immediate-release (IR) solid oral dosage forms for which bioequivalence may be assessed based on in vitro dissolution tests. (3) To recommend methods for classification according to dosage form dissolution, along with the solubility and permeability characteristics of the drug substance. According to the BCS, drug substances are classified as follows: Class I—High Permeability, High Solubility; Class II—High Permeability, Low Solubility; Class III—Low Permeability, High Solubility; and Class IV—Low Permeability, Low Solubility.

Bioresearch monitoring initiative: Bioresearch monitoring program of the FDA includes the development and implementation of compliance programs to provide guidance for inspections of investigators, sponsors, contract research organizations, institutional review boards, and bioequivalence facilities. With the expansion of clinical trial studies and sites, electronic record-keeping in the studies, and greater participation by vulnerable subjects in clinical trials, the role of FDA's bioresearch monitoring compliance programs must expand and evolve as well.

Biosimilar: A biological product that has the same physical, pharmacokinetic, and biologic properties of a patented biological product, manufactured through the same processes (e.g., plasmids, host cells, fermentation, and purification for recombinant proteins) and based on various chemical and biologic analyses; also called a biogeneric.

Biostatistics: The evaluation of statistical parameters in the conduct and analyses of preclinical and clinical studies. Also, the group at a company responsible for assisting in the designs of study protocols, especially the statistical section discussing the appropriate mathematical, medically related tests to be applied to the study data and results, and creating reports of the statistical results of clinical studies after the conclusion of a study.

Biotechnology working group (BWP): A group of experts for biological products in Europe involved in the regulation of biologicals and formally associated with the regulatory agencies.

Black box warning: In a product's labeling, a section that discusses and highlights a serious and potential adverse effect attributed to the product for substantial warnings to health care professionals and the public. The section is circumscribed by a black box.

Blockbuster: A product that sells at least $1 million per year, associated with a large patient population, an unmet medical need, a chronic disease being treated, competitive superiority in efficacy, competitive superiority in toxicity, premium pricing, global approvals (United States, European Union, and Japan), a high level of marketing spend at launch (market penetration), long patent life (over five years), and protected label extensions planned.

Board-Certified Pharmaceutical Specialist (BCPS): A healthcare professional, usually a pharmacist, who is evaluated by written examination by an independent standing board of experts to be certified as expert in a specific therapeutic and practice area.

Bonus: Cash paid to a person or company for achieving a target in their objectives, usually an annual payout; alternatives to cash are stock options or gifts for a bonus.

Box warning: In product labeling, a serious potential adverse event will be highlighted with a black box circumscribing the warning to call the health professional's attention to it and to improve product use and patient monitoring.

Brand: A product along with its official name or trade name, that is registered and associated with a particular company in a therapeutic area, plus its place in the marketplace in which it is used and sold.

Brand awareness: Recall by a customer of the product and its main use or benefit.

Brand name: Name of a single source product or manufacturer's name for multi-source product; the name created by innovator company.

Bridging study: In drug development, at least three situations warrant performance of a supplemental "bridging" study, that is, using one set of data in one study from an applicable population to extrapolate to a related but different population, in order to show similar drug responses; when the formulation changes, when adult data is being applied to a pediatric population, and when foreign data is being applied to a U.S. new drug application. The data may be pharmacodynamics, pharmacokinetic, safety, efficacy, dose and/or dosage regimen. For foreign data, ethnic factors may play a role in designing the bridging study. For a pediatric situation, pharmacokinetic or pharmacodynamic differences may need to be addressed.

Budget forecasts: The projected expected outlays of a budget in key categories over a specified time period.

Budget roll-ups: The budget is broken down into its standard categories (e.g., T/E, salary, equipment, utilities) and then can be further divided by other parameters, such as products, vendors, or studies, under which all the varied standard expenses are "rolled-up."

Bundled sale: Arrangement under which the rebate, discount, or other price concession is conditioned upon the purchase of one drug, along with drugs of different types or some other performance requirement, or where the resulting discounts or price concessions are greater than would have been available if the items were purchased separately outside the bundling.

Burden of disease (BOD): The full impact of a disease on the healthcare system and society, including all costs of care (direct and indirect) and lost productivity, all of which are usually quantified in dollars.

Business case: A plan and rationale for a new business venture, usually addressing the questions what, why, how, when, by whom, and for how much, in order to justify the new product, or program, or other initiative.

Business plan: The plans for the research, development, testing, marketing, and sales of a product, including an integrating strategy, rationale, goals, and action plans (activities, responsible party, and timeframes for completion), along with budgets, staffing, programs, and potential revenues.

Business reply card (BRC): A postcard used by companies provided to customers to order products or other materials (e.g., for education) from the company or its vendor.

Business unit (BU): A functional area in a company that is responsible for the business operations for a therapeutic area or product area, most often including sales and marketing areas and their support units (operations, staff, sales targets, and budgets). Research and development areas may be incorporated as well.

C

Call center: Telephone service to address customer questions wherein calls are centralized (in- and out-going) to one area in the company or its vendor.

Candidate: A designation for a protein, peptide, or compound that has most or all of the properties of a desired therapeutic, and is ready to move to the next stage of product development, usually from the laboratory to preclinical or clinical evaluation.

Capacity planning management: A functional area in a company that plans for physical plant, systems, and possibly staffing to meet the needs of a future expanded or new operational area.

Capitalization: Value of a company in the market (stock value), impacted by its profitability (productivity, expenses, price of products, and assets) and future potential favorable outcomes, based on investment community and public confidence. The calculation is the number of outstanding stock shares multiplied by the stock price.

Carcinogenic potential: The potential of a product to cause cancer, based on cell culture, animal, or human studies.

Case report form (CRF): Paper or electronic form designed to capture all the data from a clinical trial for each patient.

Cash flow curve: A graphic representation of cash generated by a product, that is, positive and negative cash (y-axis) above and below a baseline of 0 (break even point) over time (x-axis), through its life cycle from its time in research through approval and marketing and eventually generic substitution.

Category X drug: Drug with teratogenic effects in animal or human studies.

Causality: Judgment of adverse events associated with a product, as produced or not by the product versus some other reason; judged by a health professional reporting the AE.

Cell therapy: Use of cells, tissues, or tissue- or cell-derived products for the prevention, mitigation, or cure of disease.

Censoring data: The process for the exclusion of patient data or a full patient record, typically due to predefined criteria, because of drop-out of patients from a study or cut-off of data collection at specified study points. An example would be the last date on which patient status can be adequately assessed; any data after this point is censored and excluded from analysis.

Center for Biologics Evaluation and Research (CBER): The functional area in the FDA for the regulation of biological products and protection of public safety, especially product approvals, their manufacture and distribution, product quality, monitoring of product safety for marketed products, the marketing and advertising activities, and oversight of the companies.

Center for Devices and Radiological Health (CDRH): The functional area in the FDA for the regulation of devices and radiological products and protection of public safety, especially product approvals, product quality, their manufacture and distribution, monitoring of product safety for marketed products, the marketing and advertising activities, and oversight of the companies.

Center for Drug Evaluation and Research (CDER): The functional area in the FDA for the regulation of drug products and protection of public safety, especially product approvals, product quality, their manufacture and distribution, monitoring of product safety for marketed products, the marketing and advertising activities, and oversight of the companies.

Center for Medicare and Medicaid Services (CMS): The U.S. government division responsible for all health-related matters, including budget support to states and national patient care programs, safety of the public, health care policies, health care regulations and care guidelines, and health-related business practices.

Center for the Study of Drug Development (CSDD): At Tufts University in Boston, Massachusetts, a group that monitors the pharmaceutical and biotechnology industries involved in product research and sales and marketing. They conduct studies of the industry operation and outcomes and publish their findings. They provide educational programs related to industry operations, including best practices in strategy R&D and S&M areas.

Center of excellence (COE): A functional unit in medical institutions, or the individual full medical institutions themselves, that are considered to produce the highest level of quality of services or products. Businesses may also identify centers of excellence for their departments or business units.

Center of influence (COI): A healthcare institution (usually) that possesses a significant and leading impact on the health practices, education, or research for a defined geographic, therapeutic, or functional area, based on the expertise of their staff, quality of their operations, and excellence of their health outcomes.

Centers for Disease Control and Prevention (CDCP): The division of the U.S. government responsible for monitoring diseases, especially infectious diseases and bioterrorism, conducting epidemiologic and clinical research, creating disease related reports, and promulgating health care guidelines.

CenterWatch: A private company that tracks the pharmaceutical industry, tabulates statistics, makes observations, and publishes reports about it.

Certificate of medicinal product: In Europe, a confirmation of marketing authorization and GMP being followed by European companies permitting export of products, especially to developing countries.

Chairman of the board (COB): The person who leads the board of directors, who are the group of experienced business and science people with oversight responsibility for the company's attaining its financial, research, and personnel goals in the short and long term time periods.

Champion, product: A person with applicable expertise (science and/or business) that strongly supports the potential use of a product and its development at a company.

Change control: Part of any process that details how and when changes are to be made to improve the process.

Channel: In product distribution, it represents a group or process through which a product is distributed from a manufacturer to users of the product, for example, hospital versus retail channel.

Chaperone protein: An accessory protein that guides the movement of a molecule, especially proteins, through the cell cytoplasm between locations or organelles.

Chemical novelty rating: An assessment by the FDA of the uniqueness of the chemical nature of a new product undergoing clinical trials, which is used in the determination of a new molecular entity versus a standard product and its review status, priority versus standard.

Chemistry, Manufacturing, and Controls (CMC): In a new drug application, this section includes all the information for physical and chemical characteristics of the active ingredients of a product, manufacturing, product testing, and quality control systems (ingredients, active pharmaceutical ingredient, and final formulation).

Chief executive officer (CEO): The person who is in charge and leads a company, sets the direction and strategy, and is responsible for all functions (R&D, S&M, Manufacturing, Finance, Human Resources, Global) and all outcomes. The CEO reports to the board of directors of the company.

Chief financial officer (CFO): The person who leads the finance division of the company, consisting of accounting and finance experts responsible for financial reports, expense monitoring and control, tax calculations and reporting, and forecasting expenses and product sales. The CFO reports to the chief executive officer.

Chief information officer (CIO): The person responsible for information technology at a company, including both hardware and software, along with systems, processes, staffing, and equipment dealing with any data requirements. The CIO reports to the chief executive officer.

Chief medical officer (CMO): The person with training most often in medicine, with a medical degree and experience in patient care and clinical research, who has oversight responsibility for the company for following good clinical practices, optimal patient care goals, medical appropriateness of research goals and programs and procedures, and appropriate disease focus in the research and development and medical marketing of the company's products. The CMO usually reports to the chief executive officer.

Chief operating officer (COO): The person who leads the operations side of the company (sales, marketing, and manufacturing), insuring execution of all strategies and plans and usually is second in command of a company. The COO reports to the chief executive officer.

Chief research officer (CRO): The person who leads the research and development areas of the company, insuring execution of all product research (plans and studies) from discovery through all clinical research. The CRO reports to the CEO.

Children's Health Insurance Program (CHIP): The program is designed for families who earn too much money to qualify for Medicaid, yet cannot afford to buy private insurance for their children. CHIP coverage provides eligible children with coverage for a full range of health services including regular checkups, immunizations, prescription drugs, lab tests, X-rays, hospital visits, and more.

Chromatography: An analytical process that fractionates a drug or biologic employing separation technology and graphic data presentation, based on certain properties of the compounds (e.g., molecular size and charge), and may employ high pressure, gas, or liquid. High pressure liquid chromatography (HPLC) is one of the most common tests for drug testing due to its sensitivity, selectivity, and specificity.

Chronic toxicity: The study of the toxic and adverse effects of a product over months to years of use in animals or in humans.

Clarity: The physical characteristic of the finished formulation referring to the clearness of the liquid in the container, that is, no abnormal coloration or particulate matter.

Clearance: The calculation of the total elimination of a product from humans or animals through various excretory processes (especially kidney and liver), expressed as amount of product eliminated over a time period (e.g., mg/hour).

Clinical data: Information and statistics dealing with results from patient related studies (e.g., demographics, product doses, patient outcomes) that can be found in any publication (original research, review articles, press reports, or abstracts), study summaries, analyses of study data, scientific presentations, status reports, individual adverse experience reports, patient records, advertisements, and even promotional pieces (containing data).

Clinical data interchange: Group to develop data standards to streamline the collection and use of patient data in clinical trials.

Clinical data management (CDM): Functional group within clinical research operations at a company that is responsible for recording, storing, preparing, and processing data from case report forms derived from clinical trials. They also design the case report forms.

Clinical development plan (CDP): The compilation and integration of all phases of the clinical studies to be done in humans, including indications, objectives, types and numbers of patients, product dosing and administration (amount of product needed), outcomes desired and undesired, safety requirements, and number and types of studies, all of which comprise the application for product approval, as well as the staffing and resource requirements, timeframes for completion, and regulatory actions needed.

Clinical grant: A phase 4 clinical trial and the associated budget given to an institution and investigator to perform the study. The study's overall purposes include a significant medical issue addressed for the disease and drug, an opportunity for the company's drug to have possible benefit, and a publishable research effort. Protocol elements include disease and drug background, objectives, endpoints, design, and statistics plan. Evaluation for funding by a company includes the investigator's credentials, an estimate of sufficient and appropriate patients available, and the institution's capabilities. Budget proposals should include staffing, patient monitoring, lab tests, drug costs, statistical analysis, travel, and overhead.

Clinical hold: The FDA temporarily stops a clinical trial during its conduct prior to product approval because of some problem with the product, usually a patient safety issue or conduct problem of the study, and requests the sponsor to respond to and mitigate the problem in order to re-instate the conduct of the study.

Clinical operations plan: In the conduct of clinical studies, administrative support for the principal investigators at health care institutions performing the study, and company staff as well, requires a company plan for how it will perform various operations related to clinical trials work, such as investigator selection and training, supply of blinded drug, case report form creation and its data management, CRO selection, coordination, and communications, site monitoring (where, for what, by whom, when), site and data audits, and safety reporting.

Clinical plan: Product's potential indications, description of studies, their timelines, and responsible parties associated with clinical trials and includes additional detail for the studies, for example, patient types and individual study objectives that are not provided in development plan.

Clinical rating scale (CRS): Monitoring tools for evaluating the efficacy of products undergoing clinical trial that are subjective in nature and are scaled for levels of change, especially for psychotherapeutic products or control of disease symptoms. Primary versus secondary efficacy scales exist. Disease state specific scales usually are primary. Secondary efficacy scales are cognitive assessments excluding dementia studies, behavioral assessments, and mood components. Other secondary scales include patient self-rating scales, caregiver reports and assessments, and safety and tolerability assessments.

Clinical research associate (CRA): A person engaged in clinical research with a company that works on various aspects of clinical studies, such as study design, monitoring, data collection, investigator communications, study site visits, or audits.

Clinical research center (CRC): A research site at a medical center for intensive clinical studies, wherein patients usually require hospitalization for special testing and monitoring. The NIH has an official list of such qualified sites.

Clinical research coordinator (CRC): The healthcare professional at an investigative site for clinical studies who is responsible for coordinating all activities for the site, its patients, and its investigators, to insure good clinical practices, proper conduct of the protocol, and patient safety.

Clinical research organization (CRO): A service company separate from the manufacturer who is a vendor for performing any of the activities involved in clinical trials for a regulatory application or post-marketing. Activities may include any one or a combination of the following: protocol writing, investigators' recruitment and training, advisory boards, patients' recruitment, screening, or assignment, case report form design, institutional review board engagement, data entry, biostatistical analyses and reports, regulatory affairs services, study monitoring, site visits, investigator or patient telephone calls, lab services, electronic data capture, records retention, adverse event reporting, drug preparation, dispensing, and records, audits at the site, report writing, study or program management.

Clinical safety: Typically, the group at a company dealing with adverse event reporting in patients from trials for investigational or marketed products, from spontaneous reports from healthcare professionals or the patient and their families, and found in literature reports. Periodic reports are generated for regulatory agencies.

Clinical Safety Officer (CSO): A healthcare professional employed by a company or the FDA who is responsible for monitoring the safety of a product used in a study, larger project, or a group of studies and for assessing safety (seriousness of the adverse effects versus benefits of the product or products) in order to protect the patients and insure proper study conduct and continuation.

Clinical study report (CSR): For each clinical study, a written summary is created by the company for each protocol (its design), the results (clinical and statistical), and any conclusions to be drawn. The CSR is signed off by the principal investigator and the company study manager.

Clinical supply: The drug product used for clinical trials during investigational trials. Early clinical trials are often done with simple dosage forms (powder in bottle, simple capsule, frozen liquid) to speed entry into clinical research. Clinical trials often have specific requirements not needed for commercial product; for example, blinded studies may require tablets placed into capsules or tablets with colored coatings. Comparator products may need to be made or over-encapsulated. Placebo products that look like the active and/or comparator need to be developed. Special packaging to better ensure patient compliance may be required (e.g., blisters, bottles with use indicators). Final formulation usually is required for phase 3 trials.

Clinical trial: A research study in humans intended to discover, verify, or establish some pharmacologic, pharmacokinetic, or toxicologic action of a drug or biological product in normal or disease subjects. Clinical trial and clinical study mean the same thing.

Clinical trials agreement (CTA): This document is the legal agreement between the investigative institution and the principal investigator with the company, and usually specifies the financial arrangements for each protocol that support the conduct of a clinical trial.

Clinical Trials Application (CTA): In Europe, this application to the EMEA requests approval to initiate and conduct clinical trials following preclinical work (equivalent of an IND in U.S.).

Clinical trials material (CTM): The conduct of a clinical study requires a protocol, a drug supply for active and comparator products with recording forms, case report forms, an investigative brochure, institutional review board approvals, adverse event report forms, all of which constitute clinical trials materials.

Clinical trials operations (CTO): Activities related to conduct of clinical trials in a product's development plan at the company and at investigation sites. They involve numerous individuals, each with specific expertise (e.g., physicians, biostatisticians, clinical monitors); are labor intensive, time consuming, and expensive; are heavily regulated (e.g., FDA, HIPAA, OIG, and NIH); and require clinicians (investigators) and volunteers (patients).

Close: The final part, in time or action, of a sales call by a sales person with a customer, wherein they make the hopeful arrangement or commitment to prescribe or buy a product.

Closed formulary: List of drugs for patient use in a healthcare system, wherein no other drug can be used, requiring only drugs on the list to be prescribed.

Closed system: An environment in which system access is limited and controlled by persons with the responsibility for the records that are in the system.

Code of Federal Regulations (CFR): Documents published by U.S. government agencies that regulate an industry, as in the FDA or OIG and the pharmaceutical industry, which present proposed or new requirements, guidelines, or guidances.

Coding: Designation and categorization of an effect or adverse event related to the use of a product and based on a structured dictionary.

Coefficient of variation: A measure of the variability of data for a parameter.

Co-investigator (COI): A clinical research person at an investigative site with the appropriate medical credentials who supports and works on behalf of the principal investigator and the company in the conduct of the study. They are delegated responsibilities for the study such as patient assessment for admission, monitoring assessments, or adverse reaction reporting. They work under the supervision of the principal investigator.

Cold calls: An unscheduled contact (usually a meeting or telephone call) to a customer by a company representative.

Co-marketing: Agreement between two companies to jointly market and sell products, as well as share the revenues.

Combination product: A drug product that contains two or more active ingredients.

Commercialization: The process of marketing a product and making it available to customers, including market research, collaboration with company scientists and external advisors, promotional activity, sales forecasts, promotional programs, public relations, follow-on research activity, and educational programs.

Commercial operations: The division of a pharmaceutical or biotechnology company responsible for the marketing and sales of products, along with its support units ("commercialization").

Committee for Medicinal Products for Human Use (CMPH): In the United Kingdom, the regulatory authority for approval for marketing of products and oversight of the pharmaceutical and biotechnology industries.

Common Procedure Terminology codes (CPT): Abbreviations and numeric codes for disease categorization for billing activities by providers and healthcare institutions.

Common Technical Document (CTD): The scientific information (medical, pharmaceutical, research, and process) for filing a new drug application by a sponsor to a regulatory agency that has been harmonized for worldwide use. The main headings and content are an overall summary, non-clinical overview, clinical overview, and study reports.

Comparability protocols: The description of study designs used to compare products in clinical, pharmacokinetic, or economic trials.

Comparator: A product (usually marketed) that is used as a reference for a new product under study.

Compassionate use: Permission for patients to use a product prior to approval or at no cost because of their significant medical need (usually life saving or major medical advance) and their poor financial status.

Compatibility: A product characteristic that states it can be used with another product without primary physical interaction during their concurrent administration.

Compendia: Reference books that establish standards for products' content and quality or contain standardized information about products (product profiles and supportive research data). They are recognized for their level of expertise, independent authorship and editing, their accuracy and completeness, authorship by national professional organizations, and often used by government agencies and healthcare systems or institutions.

Competitive acquisition program: The purchase program in CMS for products, wherein the intent is to foster more product competition and lower drug prices for the U.S. government.

Competitive analysis: Market research for a product that identifies, quantifies, and analyzes the features, benefits, risks, limits, and costs of other products or treatments used for the same indication and compares them with the company's product. The capabilities of a competitor company also may be examined.

Competitive intelligence: Information collected and evaluated by one company about the products and actions of another company who markets products in the same arena.

Complaint, product: A problem with a product reported by a patient or provider to a company that involves the product's integrity, its formulation, or packaging.

Comp plan: Compensation plan to a group includes payments to individuals regarding salary, bonus, benefits, awards, and pay grades for the functional area and their differential compensation.

Complement determining region (CDR): Structural area on monoclonal antibodies that binds to a specific epitope (usually site on cell surface) that is its target antigen.

Complete response (CR): In clinical trials, most often used in oncology, a patient's disease response to treatment, wherein no evidence of disease remains for a designated period of time.

Compliance: Following accurately and completely the directions prescribed by a healthcare provider, or the protocol requirements of a study, or good clinical practices, or regulatory guidelines, or any guidance in the conduct of good research or business practices.

Compliance program guidance: This written guidance from the U.S. government addresses regulatory and legal issues in conducting medical education programs. As a guide, they are not requirements but will help avoid regulatory and legal action later if there is undue bias, inadequate independence, and inappropriate company influence on the content and conduct of educational events.

Comprehensive cancer network (CCN): The National Cancer Institute has a designated group of 27 healthcare institutions across the United States for oncology practice, education, and especially research for clinical studies and basic research in oncology, termed the National Comprehensive Cancer Network (NCCN). Specific standards in oncology and research are required for staff, resources, and capabilities. An opportunity for collaboration in research and education exists for this network.

Composition of matter: A phrase used in patent law that describes what a potential product consists of to be potentially patented.

Compound annual growth rate (CAGR): The percentage increase in a statistic calculated annually, wherein percentage growth is calculated from a changing base figure annually (up or down), which is a composite of the prior year and any growth during the year.

Confidence interval (CI): The variation for a parameter around the average (mean) on each side of the mean. A range of values that has a specified probability of containing the estimated rate or trend of interest. The 95% ($P = 0.05$) and 99% ($P = 0.01$) confidence intervals are the most commonly used.

Confidential disclosure agreement (CDA): A legal document between two or more parties that concur to keep any information shared between them for an activity, such as a protocol or consultation, confidential between the parties, usually unless both parties agree to divulge information to others. Also known as a confidentiality agreement or a Non-Disclosure Agreement (NDA).

Confounding factors: In research design for clinical or pharmacoeconomic studies, an attempt is made to control as many variables as possible and to focus on the drug being studied and specific endpoints; however, not all variables can be controlled, for example, concurrent diseases, and they become potentially "confounding" factors, that is, limits to the strength of any conclusions to be made from a study.

Conjoint analysis: Market research wherein products are compared and customers or providers are surveyed for their opinions and preferences.

Consent form: A written document requesting a patient's agreement to participate in a study. It is provided to prospective study participants and describes potential benefits/risks, alternative treatments, the study's procedures, and study events subjects will experience if they agree to participate. Their ability to stop at any time is stated. Evidence of informed consent is provided by subject's and investigator's signatures on the form.

Consolidation: A merger between and integration of two companies into one (or an acquisition of one by another) within an industry.

Consolidated Omnibus Budget Reconciliation Act: Healthcare financing legislation by federal government in 1985.

Consumer Price Index (CPI): (1) A measure of the average change in prices over time in a fixed group of goods and services. (2) The index of consumer prices for all urban and clerical customers (U.S. average) developed and updated by the U.S. Department of Labor.

Continuing education unit (CEU): A numerical value given to an educational event or program that is a postgraduate educational event (e.g., 1 CEU equals a 3-hour time commitment in a group or self-education session). An appropriately qualified educational institution establishes the CEU value of any educational event.

Continuous infusion: An administration of a product usually by parenteral or enteral routes at a steady and continuous rate over an extended period of time.

Continuous marketing application (CMA): In the NDA process with the FDA, a sponsor submits predefined portions of their marketing application at specific stages for review before submitting the completed application.

Continuous quality improvement (CQI): The business or research practices at any company can be made better in their planning, staffing, content, conduct, and evaluations to improve efficiency, accuracy, outcomes, or costs through addressing quality of their operations. Best practice companies perform routine continuous quality improvement.

Contract: A written and signed legal agreement between two or more parties for services or products that details any responsibilities and obligations, along with any financial arrangements to be met.

Contract research organization (CRO): An individual or company that serves as a vendor for a sponsor to perform some delegated role for a specific time for a specific product in its research. A whole research program, single study, or specific activity may be done by the CRO. Roles regarding research may be patient recruiting, investigator selection or training, laboratory testing, patient tissue sampling, site monitoring, data collection and recording, site visits, biostatistical analyses, and report writing.

Contract sales organization (CSO): An external vendor that provides sales personnel on a contractual basis for the company to sell its products. They may also provide other support services related to sales such as sales planning (staffing, goals, and objectives), compensation plans, and implementation.

Control article: A product that is a reference standard that is used for comparison to a new product in a study.

Controlled randomized trial (CRT): In the design of a clinical study, assignment of patients to treatment groups is done "randomly" using random number tables and includes other design features such as comparison groups and blinding of drugs.

Controlled substance: Any drug or product listed in any schedule of the Controlled Substances Act, usually related to the product's abuse record or potential. Special prescription limits, extra reporting, records keeping, and storage are required for such products.

Copyright clearance: Requests to a publisher and/or author for use of their materials in a new and different publication or use.

Corporate accounts manager (CAM): A sales person in a management position that particularly deals with large customers or customer groups, selling the company's product, assessing the customer's business and possible relationships with the company, and serving as the liaison to the company.

Cost-benefit: Ratio of cost to benefits of a product with both expressed in monetary terms.

Cost-effectiveness: Ratio of cost to benefits of a product with effectiveness expressed per unit of change in a measure, for example, mmHg of blood pressure, or in years saved and cost expressed in monetary terms.

Cost-of-goods (COG): The cost for the manufacture of the finished product, including the drug or biological manufacturing, final formulation, the container system, and the packaging and labeling, but excluding any other operating costs.

Cost-minimization: Cost of items in a by side-by-side comparison of two products assuming the same efficacy of the two products.

Cost-utility: Ratio of cost to benefits of a product with benefits expressed in quality adjusted life years saved.

Covered healthcare provider: A healthcare provider who electronically transfers any health information between two parties to carry out financial and administrative activities and claims related to health care.

Critical Path Initiative (CPI): An FDA program (new as of 2005/2006) to examine drug development and the FDA review requirements in order to expedite drug development, yet insure safety and efficacy of new treatments, for example, use of biomarkers, predictive safety testing, novel drug dosage forms, and pharmacogenomics the current CPIs for 2005–2007.

Critical success factors: The conduct of a business or research involves many components that are needed to achieve and exceed goals. A specific and limited subset of these components is especially important and essential toward achievement of goals, that is, critical success factors.

Culture: Style of work at a company, including, for example, the dress, communication and collaboration styles, approachability of senior staff, meetings (attendance, structure, and conduct), and governance.

Cure rate (CR): A term in oncology or infectious disease studies and therapy that indicates the complete response (all the tumor's physical evidence and symptoms being resolved 100% at that specific timeframe) and/or partial response (predefined major improvement in the cancer), but limited to a specified time period observed until return of the cancer. It is not 100% elimination of disease forever.

Customer: The person or institution who purchases, distributes, dispenses, administers, uses or controls a product's use, or consumes a product or service from a company, and the company tries to influence their decision about the product's use.

Cycle time: The time period in research and development of drugs in the industry from phase 1 studies start time through regulatory approval.

Cytochrome P450: A specific set of the isoenzymes in the liver that are commonly involved in the primary pathways for metabolism and degradation of drugs.

D

Data management: The department in the clinical research area of a company responsible for designing the case report forms and performing the data entry from them into the company's database.

Data management plan (DMP): A plan is usually prepared by both data management and biostatistical staff before a study starts and no later than unblinding of data. The plan describes how data will be managed (e.g., entered, transferred, and cleaned), what statistical tests are to be used in the analysis of data, and what endpoints will be measured.

Data mining: The search for information or data and their associations from an existing healthcare system, a completed study, a set of studies, or a drug research database, after the database has been created, for example, the file of studies for a new drug application for a drug with the sponsor, or the data for all the patients in a managed care organization. Often it is associated with a generation of new publications for data sets or endpoints not originally studied, but that have significant patient care or marketing value for a product. Also, it is associated with attempting to extract information from a trial (or trials) that did not meet their primary endpoints.

Data Monitoring Committee (DMC): Independent (from a company) group of scientists and individuals with the responsibility to oversee the data collected in a clinical trial to periodically assess safety and efficacy, in order to protect patients and stop a trial early if the data are compelling for excess toxicity or substantial efficacy beyond expectations.

Date of approval: The date on the letter for the final approval of the new drug application from the FDA or other regulatory agency.

15-Day Alert: An adverse reaction report by a sponsor to the FDA required to be done within 15 days of an adverse experience that is serious and unexpected.

90-Day conference: At about 90 days after filing a new drug application for all new chemical entities and major new indications, the opportunity exists for a meeting of the sponsor and the FDA. The sponsor requests the meeting with the agency. The FDA provides feedback on the status of the application and any deficiencies.

Debarment certification: In an application to regulatory authorities, the company states that no investigator in the studies has been banned by the agency from performing such studies.

Decision gates: Certain points in time and/or at certain milestones in the research and development of a product, where management needs to decide on advancing, slowing, changing, or stopping the research, based on a predetermined set of criteria.

Declaration of Helsinki: This international document intends to protect patients and human subjects who are biomedical research participants. The Declaration of Geneva of the World Medical Association binds the physician that the health of the patient will be his or her first consideration, and the International Code of Medical Ethics states that physicians will act only in the interest of the patient when providing medical care. A set of principles is established to guide the physician, researchers, and patients.

Detailing: The sales interactions, processes, and use of promotional materials for a product done by a sales person with customers.

Development: The clinical research area and studies for a product leading to an application for marketing approval. Sometimes, preclinical (animal) research and manufacturing areas are included.

Development plan: Time and events for all the major projects and milestones in the clinical research for a product by each major unit working on a product, such as clinical area, manufacturing, pharmacology/toxicology, regulatory, formulations, safety, quality assurance, stability, and package engineering. All studies for the desired package insert for a product, resource requirements, budgets, role of scientific advisory boards and focus groups, and publication plans are included.

Diagnosis related group (DRG): National standard for disease categorization with numbering system used in billing for healthcare services.

Direct-to-consumer (DTC): Advertising for a product by a company to patients or consumers directly via media, mail, television, print copy, or other means, and not through healthcare professionals.

Disability: A substantial disruption of a person's ability to conduct normal life functions.

Discipline review letter (DRL): A letter used to convey early thoughts on possible deficiencies found by a discipline review team for its portion of the pending application at the conclusion of the discipline review. The FDA does not consider discipline review letters to be action letters because they do not represent a complete review of the submission and, therefore, do not stop the user fee review clock. In addition, a discipline review letter does not necessarily reflect input from upper supervisory levels (i.e., Division or Office Directors). A single discipline review letter may contain comments from multiple discipline reviews if it is more efficient to do so. The FDA may review such information if it determines that such review would not adversely affect its ability to meet its PDUFA performance goal for that review cycle. The FDA has no obligation to review information submitted in response to a discipline review letter during the review cycle in which the discipline review letter was issued.

Disclaimer: A report or information from an applicant, sponsor, or the FDA about an adverse experience report that no conclusion is made about causality on the part of the sponsor or FDA related to the drug under study.

Disclosure: (1) Any presentation or publication of information. (2) In patenting a product, the inventor must provide publically sufficient information to allow one skilled in the art to repeat the invention.

Discount: An amount of refund or price reduction, often a percentage of the purchase, related to the sales of a product for a specific time period with a specific customer.

Discount card: A card used in healthcare systems to help patients purchase prescription drugs at a reduced cost (discount).

Discounted cash flow (DCF): Businesses that receive income from sales of products will have a flow of cash (dollars) into the company and out of the company to vendors or employees, and also the amount of cash may be reduced by a discount (percentage reduction in charges for products or services).

Discovery: Basic research that identifies disease targets and potential therapeutic compounds (hits and leads) at the laboratory stage of research.

Disease burden: An estimate of the financial, emotional, or social impact that a disease creates within the population. Different racial, ethnic, geographic, and age groups in the United States do not share the burden of disease equally.

Disease state management (DSM): A set of standardized processes and practice guidelines that provides specific alternatives in the treatment and follow-up for a disease, usually based on evidence-based medicine.

Dispensing fee: The monies collected at the point of sale of a product to cover the pharmacy costs, in excess of ingredient costs, in insuring the possession of a covered outpatient product by a Medicare or Medicaid recipient. Included activities are time for computer checks for information about coverage, drug utilization review, preferred drug list review, measurement or mixing of drugs, filling containers, beneficiary counseling, provision of product to beneficiary, delivery, special packaging, and overhead for facility and equipment.

Distribution: (1) A description, usually mathematically, of the sites and the amounts of a product that is found throughout an animal or the human body. It depends upon tissue penetration, product pharmacokinetics, tissue and plasma protein binding. It is represented as Vd, the volume of distribution in liters. For example, a Vd of 70 liters suggests distribution throughout the body of a 70 kg man. (2) The processes and sites (interim sites, such as wholesalers, or final, hospital or clinic) that a product is shipped to for purposes of eventual use in healthcare settings.

Dividend: Cash payment periodically to stockholders, based on number of shares held and the profitability of a company in a particular year or quarter.

Dose: The quantity of drug or biological that is given to a patient to achieve an expected action.

Dose limiting toxicity (DLT): An amount of drug given to an animal or patient that produces unacceptable toxic reactions substantially impacting animal or patient safety. This level of drug is the dose limiting toxicity and should not be exceeded.

Dose proportionality: The estimation or actual measurement of blood or plasma levels for a set of doses of a molecule, which can be linear (an increment in dose yields a directly proportional rise in levels) or non-linear (an increment in a dose yields a non-proportional rise in levels).

Double-blind (DB): In the design of an animal or clinical study, two treatment groups receive different products, and/or doses of a product, and/or different formulations, but both the patients and investigators do not know which patient receives which product or dose. "They are blinded."

Down round: Funding term reflecting the raising of additional capital where the stock price is the same as in the prior round of financing.

Drug: (1) A compound recognized by official pharmacopoeia or formulary as a drug, which is intended for use in the diagnosis, cure, mitigation, treatment, or prevention of disease.
(2) Small molecule organic compounds are drugs obtained by screening large libraries of natural or synthetic compounds or synthesis through medicinal chemistry, with a molecular weight typically less than 500 Daltons, produced by chemical or semi-synthetic synthesis, and effective against intracellular and extracellular targets. Examples include most antibiotics and existing pharmaceuticals.

Drug approval packages: All the information in an application to a regulatory agency for marketing authorization. The FDA reviewer comments on the data to support drug/biologic product approvals.

Drug coverage: Extent of payment to a provider or institution for the costs of drugs used by a patient, in part or in full, by a payer for the pharmaceuticals, including drug acquisition, adjunct approved services, and any overhead.

Drug development: Clinical research plans (goals, budgets, staffing, and deadlines), clinical studies, desired outcomes, milestones, and regulatory applications for a drug or biological. Sometimes, preclinical (animal) research studies are included.

Drug interaction (DI): Two or more drugs being used at the same time and resulting in some interaction between them with some added benefit, no impact, reduced benefit, or adverse outcome.

Drug master file (DMF): The information submitted to the FDA by a person who intends it to be used to incorporate the information for an IND filing, an application, an abbreviated application, an amendment, or supplement. The FDA only reviews the file in the context of an application. The information may include drug substance, drug product, materials used in its preparation (excipient, colorant, flavor, essence, or others), packaging materials, or any information used in a submission to the agency.

Drug regimen review (DRR): A process in healthcare institutions is conducted where a particular targeted treatment (a single drug product or a therapy for a target disease) is examined for a group of patients by a team of experts to determine the appropriateness of the treatment for the patients, as usually compared to some standard.

Drug review team: The FDA team members responsible to perform a drug review of the application for marketing approval, including, based on their technical expertise and data submitted, biologists, biochemists, immunologists, pharmacologists, biopharmaceutists, microbiologists, toxicologists, physicians, project managers, and statisticians.

Drug safety: An issue with the safety (adverse effect profile) of a drug recognized by the FDA, wherein a significant alteration in the risk–benefit may exist with the potential to alter physician prescribing.

Drug Safety Oversight Board (DSOB): In the FDA, an independent group to oversee management of drug safety issues for investigational and marketed products and provide information to healthcare professionals and patients about risks and benefits of medicines.

Drug substance: The active ingredient that is intended to furnish pharmacological activity or other direct effect in the diagnosis, cure, mitigation, treatment, or prevention or affect any function of the human body.

Drug utilization review (DUR): The assessment of a drug's use in a healthcare institution or system in the context of the drug's labeled and other uses, usually documenting number and type of patients; drug types, doses, their uses (approved versus unapproved), adjunctive therapies; and prescriber information for the product.

Drug Watch web site: An FDA web site wherein emerging safety information will be posted for serious side effects with drugs, even before it is fully determined that the drug is responsible for the side effect.

Dual eligible: Indigent patients who are eligible for payment for medical coverage by both the federal Medicare and state Medicaid systems.

Durable medical equipment (DME): Medical equipment used over an extended time period that is ordered by a doctor (or, if Medicare allows, a nurse practitioner, physician assistant, or clinical nurse specialist) for use in the home, such as walkers, wheelchairs, or hospital beds.

E

Early clinical trials: Phase 1, 2a, and 2b studies for a product (human studies).

Earnings per share (EPS): A fiscal statistic for companies that demonstrates a measure of profitability. Earnings are income minus any discounts and all costs of operations. Shares are company stock shares.

E-mail: Communication of memos, reports, or information over the internet (electronic mail).

Effectiveness: Overall benefit a product produces including efficacy, side effects, quality-of-life, and cost.

Efficacy: A product's extent of activity in producing the intended desirable effect.

Electronic data capture (EDC): In clinical trails, data from patient assessments, drug records, or medical tests and charts can be recorded directly into a computerized system to expedite the collection and improve the accuracy (of recording) of the data. Electronic data submission from an e-database at a patient site to a company.

Elimination: The excretion of a product from the body by all routes. Typically, quantitative elimination is measured by ^{14}C mass balance for fecal/urine/expired air excreta.

Emergency use: A test article for a human subject in a clinical trial is used in a life-threatening situation in which no standard acceptable treatment is available and time for institutional review board approval is not possible.

Enabling technologies: Processes, systems, or equipment that increases productivity or improves outcomes in the research or manufacturing of a product, for example, bioinformatics, high through-put screening, micro-array analyses, and electronic submissions of NDAs to the FDA.

End of review conference: A meeting between the FDA and the sponsor of a product about its new drug application, after the FDA has completed their review of the new drug application, and a letter of approval or non-approval has been issued.

Endpoints: The specific parameters for a disease being evaluated in a study, particularly focused on an end result that represents significant change in the disease.

Endpoints, alternative: For clinical trials, target parameters representing a disease that potentially can be improved by a product; however, they are not the historically standard disease parameters and represent new disease indicators that can be improved earlier in the course of a disease, for example, elimination of a cancer marker like an oncogene versus disease progression or survival. Examples of alternative endpoints can be biochemical endpoints, such as activation or inhibition of critical pathway enzymes, blood flow/perfusion evaluated by magnetic resonance imaging or positron emission tomography, symptom improvement, or health-related quality of life.

Endpoint, clinical: A potential and clinically meaningful change in a disease that impacts a patient's ability to feel, function, or survive.

Endpoints, surrogate: Clinical or biological parameters (e.g., cholesterol levels in blood) for a disease (e.g., coronary artery disease) under investigation that are not direct measures of the disease, but are reliable representatives of disease changes and drug actions, such that they can be used to establish and monitor efficacy of a product.

Engineering, package: Group responsible for the design and creation of a product's outer container system, such as boxes or bottles, which also must accommodate labeling needs, package insert availability, stability considerations of a product, and shelf storage.

Engineering, process: Any new development or updating of any process used at a company in any division.

Enrichment design: Improvements in study design for more desirable outcomes from a study by prospective subgroup analyses being incorporated.

Enterprise value: A financial term for a business that takes into consideration more global traits, beyond profits and losses to include quality of staff, leadership, operational efficiency, product line, and research programs. Calculation can be done with market capitalization (number of shares outstanding multiplied by stock price) plus cash minus debt; sometimes, it is further divided by total sales to better equate small and big companies.

Epidemiology studies: Observational studies in more representative disease populations of the real world, that are characterized as follows; large size, prospective or retrospective, longitudinal over specified time, well-defined hard endpoints, sites more in community versus academic settings, and use of comparator control groups. Information sources include databases, patient registries, and charts/medical histories. Goals in study of the study target disease identify and characterize risk groups, disease descriptors, and/or practice patterns. Rates of background events, for example, adverse events, are estimated. Cohort design involves a group of patients with a target disease, with and without exposure to specific products. Case control design involves a collection of individual cases of patients with a specific exposure or reaction and then selecting matched controls from same population.

Epigenetics event: Genetic change that can affect gene expression without modifying the actual sequence of DNA including phenomena such as DNA methylation (most common), RNA-associated silencing, and histone modification. An epigenetics event alters reading of the blue print.

Epitope: Structural area at a specific site usually on cell surface that is the target antigen, where a ligand can bind, often for monoclonal antibodies.

Equity interest (significant): Any ownership interest, stock options, or other financial interest whose value can not be determined, or any equity interest in a publicly traded corporation that exceeds $50,000.

Essential documents: Related to clinical studies, the principal documents that demonstrate adherence to good clinical practices and permit evaluation of the design and conduct of a clinical study by auditors, for example, investigators' brochure, protocol, informed consent form (signed), curriculum vitae of investigators, randomization list, monitoring visit reports, case report forms (signed), subject enrollment log, final report.

Establishment licensing application (ELA): An application to the FDA by a sponsor of a new product to receive approval for the manufacturing site, physical plant, equipment, processes, procedures, and first lots of a product.

Estimated acquisition cost (EAC): The estimated cost of a product or service paid by a company, or institution, or provider to a manufacturer or labeler, excluding discounts or rebates or group purchase contracts, that is, the net cost. Delivery charges may be included.

Ethical company: Pharmaceutical company that develops products from discovery through marketing, including research and development, sales and marketing, legal and regulatory, and manufacturing.

Ethical pharmaceuticals: Prescription products.

Ethics Committee: An independent group consisting of health professionals and non-medical people who are responsible to ensure that a study ensures that patients and subjects have their rights and safety, as well as, their general well-being are being protected.

Ethnic factors: Related to a population, grouped according to common traits and customs of the group. Extrinsic ethnic factors include environmental or cultural factors, such as diet, sunshine, use of alcohol or tobacco. Intrinsic ethnic factors include, for example, genetic polymorphisms, age, gender, physical traits, or organ function.

European Medicines Evaluation Agency (EMEA): The regulatory group for the European Union, harmonized across all member countries, that receives standardized marketing applications, approves product marketing, and has oversight responsibilities of the biopharma industry, including business, education, manufacturing, and research, as well as ensuring public safety.

Evidence-based medicine (EBM): The diagnosis and treatment of diseases based on published and widely accepted (by experts in the field) studies that provide the clinical data and accepted interpretations to support the clinical decisions.

Excipient: An ingredient in a solid formulation, tablets or capsules, that is not an active pharmacologic agent but adds consistency to the formulation in its manufacture and use.

Exclusivity: In the marketing and sales of a product, a company is the sole manufacturer and outlet to obtain a product during a specified period of time.

Executive committee (EC): The senior management and leadership of a company, usually including the chief executive officer, chief operations officer, chief financial officer, and division heads, such as, research and development, sales and marketing, legal, and manufacturing, who will make major company decisions, be responsible for execution of all functions, and fulfill corporate objectives.

Expanded access program: During the later clinical trials period for a new product and after showing some reasonable level of drug activity and safety, but before approval by regulatory agencies, the FDA will allow a product to be made available on a limited basis to medically qualified individual patients, restricted to emergency care products or products with a major advance in patient care for a disease.

Expectedness: Character of an adverse event related to it previously having occurred and documented versus a new unexpected event. The adverse event is information found in the labeling after product approval or investigator's brochure during research for the product.

Expert working groups (EWG): In Europe, the International Conference on Harmonization parties that develop guidelines addressing technical requirements for product development in areas of quality, safety, efficacy, and content of the common technical document.

Expert working party (EWP): Group of experts in Europe for various therapeutics or regulatory areas; for example, biotechnology, pediatrics, or vaccines, that assist with developing guidelines for product development in these areas.

Exploratory IND: A clinical research program that occurs very early in phase 1, involves very limited human exposure (up to seven days of dosing), has no therapeutic intent, and examines early toxicity issues.

Export certificate: An FDA document that allows a company to export a product (approved or not approved for marketing) to a foreign customer or government, and it attests that the product was inspected by the FDA and manufactured with current good manufacturing practices.

Export of new drugs: A new drug may be distributed outside the United States if it is subject to an approved new drug application or pertains to an investigational new drug application.

Extended release (ER): Formulation lengthening the timeframe for product delivery into the body following its administration.

Extensible markup language (XML): Automated statistical reporting system and computer language for reports, data transfer, and archiving.

Ex vivo: The study of a product outside of a living animal.

F

Family member: Spouse, parent, children, siblings, spouses of siblings, and any individual related by blood or affinity whose close association with the subject is equivalent of a family relationship.

Fast track approval: FDA approval of a new drug application or biologics license application in a shorter timeframe (6 months or less), in order to expedite development and review of drugs/biologics that are intended to treat serious or life-threatening conditions and with potential to address unmet medical needs; designated by the FDA.

FDAMA (Section 111): Originally in 1997, a federal act for the modernization of FDA drug approvals, including a 6-month marketing exclusivity extension for pediatric trials done by a sponsor, more frequent meetings between the FDA and a sponsor, for example, end of phase 2, to improve communications and expectations for studies and approval requirements. Renewal of FDAMA occurred in 2002 and 2005.

FDA advisory committee meeting: In the product approval process for a new drug application or biologics license application, the FDA forms external expert advisory groups to discuss the application, the supportive data, and the merits of product approval, including their specific recommendation, usually just prior to product approval or denial. A company presents its data and recommendations, as well as answer questions, and must prepare well for this critical meeting, that is, understand new drug application/biologics license application data, literature data, and the proposed package insert; interact frequently with reviewing Division; prepare for multiple audiences, such as the FDA, committee members, competition, public, and stock analysts; prepare committee briefing package and primary and backup slides; study backgrounds of committee members, past advisory panel hearings, politics of the open, and this public forum; and choose best presenters from the company and its investigators.

FDA Alert: FDA communication to public or healthcare professionals, regarding a safety concern with a specific product or category of products, presenting the problem, data and information about the problem, and recommended actions to be taken.

Federal Register (FR): The U.S. government publication where new policies, rules, regulations, and guidelines are published for any area of government, including oversight of health care and the research and marketing of products for patients. Usually two steps are employed; first in proposed draft form for comment by the public, science groups, business entities, and others, and second later published in final form for the respective regulated group and government agency to follow. When the new rule or regulation is final, it will appear in the Code of Federal Regulations.

Federal supply schedule (FSS): The collection of multiple award contracts used by federal agencies, U.S. territories, Indian tribes, and other specified entities to purchase supplies and services from outside vendors. Federal supply schedule prices for the pharmaceutical schedule are negotiated by the Veterans Administration and are based on the prices that manufacturers charge their "most-favored" non-federal customers under comparable terms and conditions. Because terms and conditions can vary by drug and vendor, the most-favored customer price may not be the lowest price in the market. Federal supply schedule prices are publicly available.

Federal Trade Commission (FTC): The U.S. government agency that sets policy about and regulates trade within the United States and with other countries.

Fee for service (FFS): In the payment for health care, the charges, or fees, that are reimbursed by payers for specific activities performed by a healthcare professional for a patient. The fees are the usual and customary amounts for a service without special contracts or discounting.

Field alert reports: Report from a company to the FDA regarding possible quality or labeling problems that may pose a health hazard.

Filing: Submission of materials to a regulatory authority.

Filler: Material used in the formulation of a product, especially oral forms, in addition to active ingredients, that have no other purpose than to bulk up the formulation to a practical useable size.

Final clinical study report: A document that describes the study protocol and all results from study, along with a discussion of the study in the context of broader disease management and the product's clinical development plan research plan. It is submitted to the FDA. An international guidance (ICH E3) provides necessary guidance for completing this report.

Finance division: The area of a company comprised of accounting and finance experts who are responsible for finance reports and monitoring and forecasting budgets, expenditures and sales across all company operations.

Financial disclosure: Public announcement of any compensation, equity interest, proprietary interest, significant advisory relationship, or other significant payment by a company to an investigator or educator, in order to demonstrate any relationships and the potential for conflict of interest, as well as their independence from the company.

Firewall: A barrier between the marketing and sales efforts of a company and the research or educational efforts of the company in dealing with their customers, particularly healthcare professionals. The goals of firewalls are to maintain the exchange of information with accuracy, independence, and fair balance, ensuring credibility of the information and processes. In pharmaceutical companies, the firewalls can be a variety of the following distinctions: different physical location for educational, research, and information groups; different review processes for medical letters, research and educational grants, and study protocols without marketing influence; compensation package and any bonuses separate from sales outcomes; standard operating procedures that detail the independence and fair balance; separate sales and marketing versus research and development organizations; a paper trail being maintained for auditors demonstrating the firewalls' function; and the employees in research and education with the appropriate credentials as health and education professionals, along with hiring and promotion independent from marketing, and a distinct budget and budget process from marketing.

First-in-class (FIC): The first product approved for use by regulatory authorities in a specific class of compounds, usually based on its pharmacology or therapeutic use.

First-in-man (FIM): The first study of a product in humans.

Fixed dose combination: Two or more drugs in designated specific amounts in one formulation constituting a final product.

Follow-on product (FOP): The marketing and sales of a new, but not novel, product that comes from the same pharmacological, chemical, or therapeutic family of the first product approved earlier for marketing in the same family.

Food and Drug Administration (FDA): The U.S. government agency responsible for the monitoring of research, the approval, and the post-approval monitoring of all new drugs (prescription and over-the-counter), biologics, devices, and foods ensuring public safety and the efficacy, safety, and quality of the products used in health care. They create regulations for the industries that provide these products to meet these goals, especially the research, approval requirements, and marketing practices.

Forced degradation: The assessment of how a product, especially the active ingredient, will breakdown (e.g., hydrolysis, oxidation, light sensitivity) under storage and handling conditions at purposefully elevated conditions, for example, temperature. It helps show analytical methods indicating stability. It provides information for manufacturing process and packaging requirements.

Forecasting: Evaluation of the potential sales by finance and marketing, or potential budgets and staffing needed for a product or functional area, or progress in research by project planners.

Formulary: Limited list of products approved for use in an institution.

Formulation: The final form of a product, for example, tablet, injection-liquid, or lyophilized. The goals are to deliver consistently active ingredients to intended sites of action in amounts required over desired time course; make an easily manufactured, reproducible product that can be made at commercial scale and with low cost of goods; produce a product that is chemically and physically stable for an acceptable shelf-life (2 to 4 years is common); offer patients and providers a convenient-to-use product; differentiate product from the competition; and create a product formulation with benefits allowing premium pricing for the value provided.

Freedom of information (FOI): A law that requires the U.S. government to give out certain information to the public when it receives a written request. Freedom of Information Act applies only to records of the Executive Branch of the federal government, not to those of the congress or federal courts, and does not apply to state governments, local governments, or private groups.

Fulfillment: Providing materials or products from the inventory of a company to a customer or internal department.

Full prescribing information: A phrase that indicates the complete package insert information is being provided.

Full time equivalent (FTE): (1) An employee or staff member who works a 40-hour week. (2) more than one person, all of whom are combined to equal the work time and output of one full-time person.

Fully integrated pharmaceutical company (FIPCO): A business enterprise in the biopharma industry that manufactures products, researches for new products, and performs sales and marketing functions, along with the various support units, such as human resources, financial operations, legal, medical affairs, and possibly also international operations.

G

Gantt style chart: A methodology to track events and times in management of a project, program, study, or group of studies, listing the major events, expected and then actual start times, expected and then actual completion time, in a single tabular, chart fashion.

Gap analysis: Market research or organizational analysis that identifies missing information, activities, people, processes, or systems needed to perform some function or market a product.

Gate-keeper: Persons or institutions in the healthcare system that are involved in decisions that can facilitate or limit access to and use of a product.

General and administrative costs: In the conduct of business at a company, costs that are outside of research and development, manufacturing, and sales and marketing are lumped together as general and administrative costs.

Generalizability: The outcomes of a study deal with a sample of patients from a much larger population. The design of the study should demonstrate that the sample was representative of the population and the outcomes can be extrapolated to the population.

Gene therapy: The identification of diseases and the responsible gene, related to abnormal or absent gene function, and the use of the gene as a therapeutic agent to correct the disease by delivering the gene directly to patients.

Genome: The collection of all the genes for an organism.

Genotoxicity: The toxic action of a product on the genetic make-up of an organism leading to damage of or mutation to genetic material.

Generic: Equivalent product in its structure, actions, product quality, and pharmacokinetics.

Genetically modified organism (GMO): A cell or animal in which the genetic make-up has been altered by adding or deleting genetic material to create a new organism that produces a new product, as in a better food stuff (more yield or more nutritional value), or as in animals who can produce human proteins.

Genetic polymorphisms: Gene alterations, additions, omissions, or deletions that alter biologic functioning or changes in drug metabolism.

Global: International focus for a plan or organization beyond the country of origin of the company.

Good clinical practices (GCP): A set of behaviors, processes, and actions by persons performing clinical studies that are intended to ensure integrity of clinical data on which product approvals are based, and to help protect rights, safety, and welfare of human subjects. Both FDA regulations and EMEA guidelines govern conduct of trials involving human subjects. Good clinical practices elements include institutional review board review and approval, informed consent, qualifications of investigators, adequate sponsor oversight, scientifically sound clinical protocols, and documentation of study conduct.

Good laboratory practices (GLP): A set of behaviors, processes, and actions by persons performing laboratory research that are intended to establish standards for conduct and reporting of non-clinical laboratory studies and to ensure quality and integrity of safety data submitted to the FDA. Good laboratory practices are required for selected, but not all laboratory studies. Good laboratory practice elements include personnel qualifications, including Study Director and Quality Assurance unit, facilities for animal care, test article control and specimen control, equipment maintenance and calibration, appropriate standard operating procedures for all aspects of non-clinical study conduct, and documentation of study conduct.

Good manufacturing practices (GMP): A set of behaviors, processes, and actions by persons performing the manufacture of a product that are intended to ensure that minimum manufacturing standards are adhered to, thereby helping to ensure the quality of drug products produced and/or sold in the United States. They are required for all drug products intended for human consumption. Good manufacturing practice elements include organization and personnel, building and facilities, equipment, controls of components and drug product containers and closures, production and process controls, packaging and labeling controls, holding and distribution, laboratory controls, records and reports, and returned and salvaged product.

Good regulatory practices (GRP): A set of behaviors, processes, and actions by persons involved in interactions with regulatory authorities that are intended to ensure optimal interactions and communications between the regulatory agencies and sponsors in the development and marketing of products, in meeting all standards, guidances, regulations, and laws regarding the regulation of products, and to ensure optimal applications to the regulatory agencies leading to product and labeling approvals.

Good review practices (GRP): A set of behaviors, processes, and actions by regulatory persons that are intended to ensure appropriate processes, procedures, communications, and documentation in the review of regulatory applications to authorities, ensuring safety, efficacy, and quality of products being approved, protecting public safety, ensuring appropriate and sufficient documents being used, and fostering efficient reviews.

Grants: Financial support for research or educational projects from a company to a customer.

Gray: Measure of radiation, absorption of 1 joule of radiation energy by 1 kg of matter.

Gross domestic product (GDP): The output of goods and services in a country quoted in a particular currency (e.g., dollars or euros) without any adjustments, for example, for inflation or value of the currency relative to others.

Gross margin: The financial figure for the difference between all revenues and costs of goods sold.

Group purchase organization (GPO): Institutions banding together to purchase pharmaceuticals, services, and other products, providing greater purchasing power that can permit optimal pricing being negotiated for the group of institutions for the products and services with the vendor.

Guidance documents: Official actions announced in writing and generated by the Center for Drug Evaluations and Research and the Center for Biologics Evaluation and Research of the FDA that span scientific issues to administrative procedures in the research, manufacturing, and application for products, and that suggest appropriate methods, processes, content, and actions for sponsors and investigators.

H

Half-life: Time for one-half of the amount of a product to be eliminated from a body, usually measured by the blood or plasma concentration decreasing by 50%.

Harmonization (ICH): International effort among world-wide regulatory agencies to streamline drug development through standardized procedures and records across countries.

Hatch-Waxman Act: Drug Price Competition and Patent Restoration Act of 1984 (Public Law 98-417) primarily intended to facilitate generic drug approvals.

Healthcare professional (HCP): A person who is trained in the medical and pharmaceutical sciences and provides care to patients to diagnose and mitigate their disease improving their health, such as physicians, nurses, pharmacists, dentists, and therapists (physical, occupational, psychiatric).

Health care utilization (HCU): The study of the use of any individual or group of products or services dealing with disease management in patients by institutions or providers.

Health economics (HE): The examination of all the costs and outcomes related to an individual or group of products and services dealing with disease management for a target disease, within an institution or health system.

Health and Human Services (HHS): The U.S. department responsible for execution of the regulations and laws addressing health care and the preservation of public health and safety.

Health Insurance Portability and Accountability Act (HIPAA): A congressional act that created requirements for the protection of private information about patients in any health-related activity including and especially access, for example, to insurance information, patient medical records, and clinical research.

Health maintenance organization (HMO): A healthcare institution or group of institutions that provides a broad scope of healthcare services with some measure of standardization of the health care, with a level of quality measured against some standard, in order to be cost-effective and provide consistent quality care.

Health savings account (HSA): A fund that an employee puts a percentage of his or her salary or savings into that is specifically and only targeted to payment for healthcare services for themselves and family members.

Health services research: A form of research about use of products or services that addresses a more complete picture of all the various outcomes beyond product safety and efficacy, such as quality of life, and all the related direct and indirect costs.

Health technology assessments (HTA): Various therapeutic options are compared and contrasted by the Center for Medicare and Medicaid Services (or a healthcare system) to determine cost-effectiveness relative to outcomes.

High technology formulary: A list of products and services that involve very specialized technologies and that are high cost items as well, which are usually controlled in their use to a higher degree than other formulary items.

High-throughput screening (HTS): Laboratory processes intended for more, high-quality product leads to be identified much faster, requiring miniaturization, automation, and new technologies in product analysis (surface chemistry [chips], capture agents, and detection methods). Prior analytic processes allowed 100 to a few 1,000 wells done/day, as compared to compound screening of more than 500,000 in a few days with high-throughput screening.

Historical control: A group of patients, subjects, or animals in a study previously treated and observed outside of the current study, along with data having been collected previously, who serve as a comparison group to the newly treated subjects.

Hit: A compound being screened in an early phase of drug discovery process that demonstrates some activity in the pharmacology test system. A test protein, peptide, or compound that appears to act on targets.

Honorarium: Payment to person for services rendered, usually a specific educational or advisory role over a limited period of time.

Hotline: Telephone system, usually toll free and expedited, for patient or customer inquiries to a company.

Human resources (HR): The division of a company responsible for personnel issues including job descriptions, training, promotion and advancement guidelines, salary and benefit policies and programs, and recruiting, hiring, and firing actions. All functions are performed with guidance from the respective expert groups in all the functional areas, such as research and development and sales and marketing.

I

Immunotoxicity: Studies evaluating immunologic effects of a product that are adverse events.

Import of new drugs: A drug received from outside the United States is permitted if it is the subject of an approved new drug application or pertains to an investigational new drug application, or is a drug substance to be used in the manufacture, processing, or repackaging of a new drug.

Incidence: Frequency of occurrence of an event in a study or over a certain time period.

Incidence rate: The ratio of the number of newly diagnosed patients of a specific disease occurring in a specified population during a year to the number of individuals who were at risk for the given disease, generally expressed as the number of cases per 100,000 persons.

Indication: The therapeutic use of a product found in the product labeling, either approved for use by regulatory agencies, and/or an unapproved use but supported by clinical data in the literature.

Inducer: A compound or molecule that stimulates an enzyme, usually in the liver, to increase the metabolism of other products metabolized by the same enzyme. A receptor may be up-regulated by one product to respond to a greater extent by a second product.

IND safety report: A sponsor of an investigational new drug must submit to the FDA and all investigators any serious adverse event that is unexpected and "associated with use of the drug" within 7 days of any unexpected fatal or life-threatening experience and within 15 days for all other safety reports.

Information management: The systems, processes, staffing, and equipment at a company for all information coordination, processing, analyses, storage, and use.

Information technology (IT): All the systems, equipment, processes, and staff to find, store, manipulate, analyze, report, and communicate information.

Informed consent: Permission given by a patient to an investigator and institution to be a subject in a clinical study, wherein they are given full information about the study, including treatments, alternatives, potential adverse events, potential benefits, any costs or cost savings, their rights (e.g., to stop their participation at any time), any consequences, contact persons, and confidentiality. This consent must be written, signed, and witnessed.

Inhibitor: A compound or molecule that decreases the activity of an enzyme, usually in the liver, and decreases the metabolism of other products metabolized by the same enzyme. The activity of a receptor stimulated by one product may be similarly diminished by the concurrent use of another product.

Initial public offering (IPO): A private company changes its status for the first time to a public company by offering ownership to others through stock purchases that are shares of ownership in the company.

Injunction: Civil action by a regulatory authority to stop production or distribution of a product in violation of regulations or drug laws.

In-licensing: Acquisition of a product from outside of a company along with the patent rights for the product.

In-process control: During the manufacture of a product or the conduct of some procedure, steps are incorporated that help to ensure the quality of the final product or outcome.

Inquiry review letter (IRL): A request or search for information by a person or agency (public or private) either inside or outside the company.

Inquiry Letter (IR): An inquiry letter is a letter sent to an applicant by the FDA during an application review to request further information or clarification that is needed or would be helpful to allow completion of the discipline review. The FDA does not consider inquiry letters to be action letters because they do not represent a complete review of the submission and therefore do not stop the user fee review clock. As with discipline review letters, an inquiry letter does not necessarily reflect input from upper supervisory levels; however, inquiry letters are not like discipline review letters in that FDA issues inquiry review letters while the discipline review continues. Information requested in inquiry review letters should be information that would assist in the completion of the review and, as such, would usually be reviewed during the review cycle in which the inquiry letter was issued.

Inspections (GMP): Pre-approval inspection or post-approval inspection for surveillance of good manufacturing practices at a company by a regulatory authority.

Inspections (for GCP, GAP, GMP, GRP, etc): Inspection of clinical sites or inspection of animal testing facilities, respectively, by a regulatory agency for adherence to the written practices in the guidance. The inspection process may or may not be announced. Site receives "Notice of Inspection." Inspector's observations are recorded on Form FDA 483, Establishment Inspection Report (EIR).

Inspection (FDA) classes: FDA findings after an inspection of the company or its vendors or investigators; NAI, no action indicated; VAI, voluntary action indicated; OAI, official action indicated.

Institution: Any public or private entity or agency. Facility is used as a synonymous term.

Institutional ethics board (IEB): A multidisciplinary group of individuals, including clinicians, researchers, public members, and often clergy, who are responsible on behalf of an institution to review and approve studies involving patients, ensuring patient's protection regarding local, national, and international standards of ethics.

Institutional review board (IRB): Institution-based group that serves important role in protection of rights and welfare of human research subjects, and has been formally designated to review and monitor research involving humans. An institutional review board has authority to approve, require modifications, or disapprove clinical research. An institutional review board approves protocols or any amendments to protocols.

Integrated health system (IHS): A healthcare institution that incorporates various products and services in the health care of their patients.

Intellectual property: A product, the scientific process to create the product or family of products, a brand name, a new formulation of an older product, a new analytical process, a new product discovery platform, any of which can be considered novel and can be patented to protect from unlawful copying by someone else.

Interactive voice response system (IVRS): Assignment of patients to drug treatments for a study by automated telephone system.

International Conference on Harmonization (ICH): An on-going international group from the regulatory authorities of Europe, Japan, and the United States and experts from the pharmaceutical industry in the three regions that discuss scientific and technical aspects of product registration and creates new standards and guidelines. The purpose is to make recommendations on ways to achieve greater harmonization across the world in the interpretation and application of technical guidelines and requirements for product registration to reduce or obviate the need to duplicate the testing carried out during the research and development of new medicines.

International unit (IU): A measure of a product's desired pharmacologic activity, based on a standardized specific assay system in animals or in vitro tests.

Intra-arterial (IA): Administration of a pharmaceutical product directly into an artery.

Intra-articular (IA): Administration of a pharmaceutical product into the synovial cavity of a joint.

Intra-dermal (ID): Administration of a pharmaceutical product into the skin.

Intramuscular (IM): Administration of a pharmaceutical product through the skin and subcutaneous tissues into the muscle at the site of injection.

Intra-peritoneal (IP): Administration of a pharmaceutical product into the peritoneal cavity or peritoneum via a catheter or syringe.

Intravenous (IV): Administration of a pharmaceutical product directly into the bloodstream through a vein.

Intra-ventricular (IV): Administration of a pharmaceutical product into a ventricle of the brain through a catheter or syringe.

Investigational device exemption (IDE): The application to the FDA by a sponsor for the marketing approval for a device to be used in patients establishing its actions and benefits, safety in patients, quality, how it operates, and operating guidelines to practitioners in its use.

Investigational New Drug application (IND): The document from a sponsor to the FDA requesting permission to initiate human studies. It includes an introductory statement, general investigational plan, investigator's brochure, study protocol(s), investigator, facilities, institutional review board data, chemistry, manufacturing, control data, animal pharmacology and toxicology data, and any previous human experience.

Investigator: A health professional or scientist who is responsible for and conducts a study of a product in a target population or laboratory study on behalf of a sponsor or manufacturer.

Investigator's brochure (IB): An extensive document for a product prior to marketing approval that summarizes a drug's (or related drugs if none available) safety, efficacy, pharmacology, toxicology, pharmacokinetics (animals and humans), risks and side effects to be anticipated, and all the research, based on the company's studies and published literature, and is provided to all investigators studying the company's drug.

Investigator-initiated trials (IIT): Studies created by investigators outside of the company requesting use of the product and funding by a company for the research. Goals will explore different uses, doses, or patients. Subsets explore basic physiologic and pathophysiologic mechanisms, and expand the investigator pool, including thought-leaders. In order to conduct such trials, specific investigator and manufacturer requirements are fulfilled, including an Investigator IND (that is referenced to the company file) and progress reports to FDA and the company. Company may assist with study design and adverse event reporting, may provide drug, and may provide funding.

Investigator records: For a study, the principal investigator or sub-investigators at sites of multicenter studies must keep documents in storage, retained for two years, and available for audits, such as drug disposition, study reports, and patient case histories (case report forms and supportive documentation).

Investigator reports: For studies, the investigator shall create and maintain progress reports, safety reports, final reports, and financial disclosure reports.

Investor relations (IR): A department at a company responsible for communications (telephone calls, letters, articles, and financial reports) with the investment communities and stockholders.

In vivo : A use or study being performed in, or a molecule or product being used in, a living organism.

In vitro: A use or study being performed outside of a living organism, usually in a laboratory setting.

Isoform: A specific and distinct structure or form of a biological molecule among a family of biological molecules with very similar structures and comparable, but not necessarily equal, actions for the same product.

Isomers: One molecule in two mirror image forms, one right-handed and one left-handed image in three-dimensional structure. The two stereoisomers can have very different pharmacological profiles.

J

J-code: Healthcare (government) procedural coding system assigning numbers for billing for specific healthcare services.

K

Key opinion leader (KOL): Influential healthcare professional, official, or administrator on current medical practice, research, or education, who is capable of inspiring peers to improve patient outcomes through their recognized research excellence, scientific literature credentials, or clinical expertise, and has an esteemed position at a leading medical or research institution.

Known side effects: Predictable adverse events based on the drug's labeling (particularly the package insert), whether avoidable or not.

L

Label: Approved information by a regulatory authority placed in a product's package insert, some of which also is found on the physical packaging, including at least the names, description, indications for use, side effects, warnings, precautions, pharmacology and toxicology, dosage and administration, formulation, how packaged, and the manufacturer.

Label claims: The FDA-approved uses, benefits, and limits of the drug, which can be found in package insert, such as disease indication (what the drug is intended to treat), target population (ages or groups who need the drug), route of delivery (IV injection, oral, nasal, etc.), potential observed benefit (the improvement seen in clinical trials), and safety issues (any toxicities noted in animals and humans).

Large simple trials: The clinical studies for a product that are done after marketing approval that collect larger numbers of patient, with fewer design controls in place, in order to obtain more realistic data on product use in typical patients in typical healthcare settings.

Late clinical trials: Studies in humans that are at phase 3, 3b, or 4 stages of product development.

Launch: Process and activities of initial marketing and sales, as well as support services, for a product associated with its regulatory approval, usually during the 2 years before and two years after approval, for example, launch "event," training, market research, field (sales) readiness, introductory ads, sales plan roll-out, key customer engagements, speakers programs, medical education, distribution, contracts, phase IV trials, and direct-to-patient advertising.

Lead: A compound in the discovery phase of research that demonstrates activity in a biological system or animal. Among numerous hits or variants, the protein, peptide, or compound showing highest degree of activity.

Lead identification: Process by which potential therapeutics found to have preliminary activity on a target for a disease, whether drugs or biologics, are screened further for pharmacologic activity and prioritized. It utilizes knowledge of the specific target to identify/design an appropriate agonist/antagonist.

Lead optimization: The compound in a biologic area or new pharmacologic category in which its structure and characteristics are being improved to enhance its desired activity, lessen its toxicity, improve its stability, and/or improve its manufacturing.

Lead validation: Process by which actions of a product on diseases is confirmed in additional animal models of a target disease.

Leader profile (Ideal by Goldsmith): Think globally, anticipate opportunities, appreciate cultural diversity, build partnerships (teams), develop technological savvy, encourage constructive dialogue, and share leadership.

Legally authorized representative: An individual, or judicial or other body authorized under applicable law, to give consent on behalf of a prospective subject to the subject's participation in the procedures involved in research.

The Leapfrog Group : An initiative driven by organizations that buy health care who are working to initiate breakthrough improvements in the safety, quality, and affordability of healthcare for Americans. It is a member-supported program aimed at mobilizing employer purchasing power to alert America's health industry that big leaps in healthcare safety, quality, and customer value will be recognized and rewarded. The Leapfrog Group was founded by a small group of large employers, initially supported by the Business Roundtable and launched in November 2000. Leapfrog is supported by the Business Roundtable, The Robert Wood Johnson Foundation, Leapfrog members, and others. The Leapfrog Group's growing consortium of Fortune 500 companies and other large private and public healthcare purchasers provide health benefits to more than 37 million Americans in all 50 states; Leapfrog members and their employees spend tens of billions of dollars on health care annually. Leapfrog members have agreed to base their purchase of health care on principles that encourage provider quality improvement and consumer involvement.

License: Approval document to market a product from a regulatory authority.

Licensing and Acquisitions (L&A): Product acquisition from a source outside of the company (university or other company) including the marketing, usually research, and patent rights, in return usually for financial compensation (e.g., milestone payments, future royalties).

Life cycle: Phases of product evolution from research through clinical research to launch and early marketing (growth phase), then on to later marketing (mature phase), second indications, new formulations and follow-on products stage, up to its generic substitution stage or later.

Life cycle management (LCM): The management process for a product's life cycle, including the staged outcomes, along with the decision criteria, players, and processes throughout research and marketing of a product.

Life-threatening: A patient or subject is at immediate risk of death from the drug, in the view of the investigator or health care provider.

Ligand: A molecule that binds to a receptor of a cell.

Linear analog scale (LAS): An assessment system of patient outcomes, usually by the patient themselves, that uses a straight line, usually 10 cm in length, with extremes in outcomes demarking the ends of the line, for example, pain linear analog scale from none to worst ever pain, wherein the patient marks on the line their assessment at a point in time.

Listed drug: A new drug product that has an effective approval for safety and effectiveness and listed in the current edition of the FDA's "Approval Drug Products with Therapeutic Equivalence Evaluations."

Locked database: Database created from case report forms for a study is secured ("locked") to prevent any further additions, changes, or deletions from being made. Analysis of the data then can proceed for the study.

Long range plan (LRP): A business practice that looks beyond the current year, most often over five- or ten-year periods, for the planning of any business component, such as sales, manufacturing, or research.

Lot release: A process for a batch of a product recently manufactured at a company, where it is first put on hold to fully analyze its quality (e.g., purity, homogeneity, product concentration), and then accepted for meeting the standards for the product and its formulation, wherein it then is allowed to be used for commercial purposes and distributed.

Lyophilization: A process for storage of products to increase the shelf-life, wherein usually the liquid formulation is freeze dried (use of heat, freezing, and vacuum for extraction of water) into a friable mass that later must be reconstituted with a diluent for the drug's administration.

M

Managed care organization (MCO): A healthcare system in which patients receive outpatient care, and also in-patient care, from healthcare providers, wherein the care is adjusted and controlled with, for example, formal practice standards, referral processes among providers, cost controls, formularies limiting drug use, and quality care standards. The managed care organization may also contract with an employer to be a payer for the health services.

Manufacturer: (1) Any entity that possesses legal title to the National Drug Code for a drug, device, or biological product. (2) The innovator company, or their licensee, or the current owner of the patent that is engaged in the production, preparation, compounding, conversion, or processing of drugs or biologicals; or may be a packager or repackager, or labeler or relabeler, but not a wholesaler or retail pharmacy.

Market: A market can be usually a disease area, a therapeutic class, pharmacologic class, or medical discipline, wherein products are purchased and used and collectively includes all the products, the patients, the providers, all people involved, and healthcare systems, as well as all related activities.

Market analysis: The assessment of the opportunity for a product's use in a disease or therapeutic area, including, for example, disease description, patient traits, drug choices, doses, and amounts, competitive products to a new product, potential uses of the new product, barriers to product use, and prescribers and influencers.

Market cap: A measure of the value of a company based on the calculation of the stock price multiplied by the outstanding number of shares for a publicly held company.

Marketing application: A filing with a regulatory authority for a new drug, device, or biological product for approval to market.

Marketing authorization application (MAA): The application in Europe to the European Medicines Evaluation Agency regulatory authority to establish a product's safety, efficacy, and quality leading to marketing approval.

Market capitalization: A measure of the value of a company based on the calculation of the stock price multiplied by the outstanding number of shares for a publicly held company.

Market potential: The size of the opportunity for the use and sales of a product in a disease or therapeutic area, usually quantified in sales dollars, or product units, or number of patients addressable by the product.

Market research: The group of studies of a product and its intended uses to identify the customer(s) and unmet needs, identify new opportunities, understand the buying process, recognize barriers to adoption and decision processes, determine the influencers and thought leaders in research and practice, determine how to ensure access, and identify the drivers of value, patient needs and behaviors, communication and promotional challenges, competitive perceptions, and positioning. The process includes exploring products and attitudes, product positioning, concept development, message testing, second creative executions in ad testing, analysis, and adjustments. Results are analyzed with perceptual mapping, gap analyses, trade-off analyses, market segmentation, and market simulation modeling.

Market segmentation: The division of a target product category, disease, or therapeutic area, dividing a market into several portions depending on selected characteristics of the category, disease, or therapeutic area (e.g., prescribers, channels, patient subsets).

Master cell bank: The new genetically-modified cells resulting from the biotechnology manufacturing processes of recombinant DNA or monoclonal antibody technologies and responsible for the manufacture of the biological products. The genetically modified organism's new cells are stored as the master cells for subsequent extraction of daughter cells, and manufacture of lots of product.

Meaningful therapeutic benefit: The drug represents a significant improvement in the treatment, diagnosis, or prevention of a disease, compared with marketed products adequately labeled for that relevant population (e.g., more efficacy, less adverse effects, enhanced compliance, and new subpopulation).

Mechanism of action (MOA): The specific type of pharmacological action of a product on a physiological system, disease pathogenesis, or disease target.

Medical affairs (MA): The department in a company responsible usually for customer interactions and internal technical support, including medical information (on-label and off-label issues), triage of customer inquiries (public, patients, providers, payers, investors, and press), medical education, marketing support (technical input and oversight), sales training (technical and clinical), medical science liaisons, and phase 4 clinical research. Also, called Professional Services at some companies.

Medical communications (MC): Information and/or education being provided by a company to external or internal customers. Activities can include publication planning of research and development trials; compendia support with research and development trials and data; sales and marketing support for thought-leader programs, speaker training, advisory boards, investigator meetings, and scientific meeting support; research and development data being identified and interpreted, especially competition, plus scientific and sales tool development (technical review), and field sales training for scientific information.

Medical education (ME): Programs to educate healthcare professionals in the medical use of a product, that need to be fair balanced, unbiased, independently designed and conducted by health care professional and institutions form a company

Medical information (MI): The unit at a company serving as the customer contact center for their inquiries about company products (telephone, e-mails, fax, and written), for providers, patients, and many others. Labeled and off-label information is provided based on data available and evidence-based medicine. Triage of inquiries is done for adverse events to the safety group, product complaints to quality assurance, patients for trials to development, reporters to public relations, investors to investor relations, lawyers to legal, reimbursement to such specialists, and competitive intelligence to marketing. Standard letter generation is done for responses as needed. Other responsibilities can include scientific publication tracking, scientific meeting support, disease state management, research questions to be addressed, patient registries, and Web-site products and questions.

Medical marketing: Educational materials as part of marketing-related materials for a product.

Medical science liaison (MSL): Medical healthcare professionals associated with a company geographically based near key customer accounts; corporately aligned based on therapeutic area, product, or account type; focused on key opinion leaders, providers, educators, and payers; involved in access to local educational grants, access to company and investigator initiated clinical studies, investigator meetings; provide scientific literature and education, speaker updates and training.

Medical writing group: A department at a company that writes reports in the research and development division, most often final clinical study reports or publications emanating from clinical studies.

Medicare, Part A: Medicare coverage primarily for hospital payments, also some nursing care, home care, and hospice.

Medicare, Part B: Medicare coverage primarily for physician services and other outpatient service providers; some drug coverage, such as oral cancer drugs, epoetin for end-stage renal disease, and beta-interferon for multiple sclerosis.

Medicare, Part C: Medicare-managed care programs.

Medicare, Part D: Medicare prescription drug benefit, approved in 2003.

Medication error: A problem with use of a medicine in patients that usually involves incorrect dosage, inappropriate administration (route, time of day, rate, or diluents), or wrong drug being used.

Medication therapy management program (MTMP): The Centers for Medicare and Medicaid Services has created a program to address and improve the outcomes, quality and efficiency, and reduce costs of medication therapy for particular diseases, wherein the costs are high, the treatments are more complicated, and the adversity in patients is relatively higher. The management program involves new types of providers and systems to achieve the improvements in conjunction with existing health providers and systems.

Medicinal chemistry: The discipline in laboratory research that creates new drug molecules and identifies and modifies the function and especially the structure of a drug or molecule (its chemistry) to obtain a desirable therapeutic agent.

Medical alert: A serious adverse event that is new in regard to its severity, frequency, novelty, or duration, and necessitates a company to formally inform the FDA, the healthcare community, and the public.

MedWatch: An FDA system for voluntary reporting of adverse experiences, product quality problems, and product-use errors with marketed products by individual providers or institutions, as well as a system for rapid communication from FDA to healthcare providers, institutions, associations, and the public about such problems.

MedWatch Form 5400: Official standard form to record adverse events and report to FDA.

Merger: Joining of two companies who combine their businesses and create a new single company.

Metabolism: Study of a drug's elimination from the body via liver by in vitro methods, such as metabolic stability, Cytochrome P-450 (CYP) enzyme inhibition/induction, metabolite identification, or in vivo methods, such as, 14C mass balance, drug–drug interaction. Liver metabolism is mediated by CYP isozymes: 1A1/2, 2D6, 3A4, 2C8/9/19. Genetic polymorphisms of CYPs and drug–drug interactions are common sources of variability. Drugs may be metabolized by more than one enzyme. Drug may induce/ inhibit one isoenzyme but may not be its substrate. Inhibition or induction of an interacting drug may or may not result in clinically significant interaction

Microarray: Analytical processes in which very large numbers of wells on a plate in very small volumes are used for analysis to identify molecules and/or determine their concentrations in samples in a facilitated process.

Microbial activity: A description of biochemical actions of the drug on microbial physiology, antimicrobial spectra of the drug, and possibly any known mechanisms of resistance to the drug, along with the clinical microbial laboratory methods needed for effectiveness determination.

Modeling: An artificial statistical and/or biological construct for a naturally occurring physiological, pharmacological, or biologic system in order to determine or estimate its function in vitro.

Molecular engineering: The structural alteration of a biological molecule to improve its actions as a therapeutic product, reduce its side effects or immunogenicity, create a more stable molecule in vivo or in vitro (storage), simplify or reduce cost of its manufacture, raise the yield in its manufacturing, or create a new patentable molecule. For example, a protein can have modifications in number and type of amino acids, the disulfide bridges, the terminal amino or carboxyl groups, glycosylation, truncation (smaller molecule), fusion of two molecules, and isoform make-up.

Monitoring: The evaluation of investigational sites for adherence to protocols and good clinical practices, which also is required under FDA/CFR regulations and is performed by the investigational new drug sponsor. Examples of practices to be evaluated are investigator following protocol, subjects being informed of study and providing informed consent, data collected accurately and recorded, drug being stored, prepared and accounted for, and study documents maintained.

Monitoring site visit: The actual meeting at the site a study is being conducted, and is done at usually four types at key landmarks in the conduct of a study; pre-study site visit (Are they qualified?), initiation site visit (Are they ready?), interim monitoring visit (Is study being conducted according to good clinical practices?), and close-out site visit (Has all necessary activities been done according to good clinical practices and is documentation in order?).

Morbidity utilization evaluation (MUE): An assessment (study) of a group of patients or a group of drug orders in a healthcare system for the occurrence of specific disease traits or adverse events.

Multi-center trial: A single protocol of a study for a product that is conducted at more than one investigative site.

Multi-variate analysis: Statistical analyses that take into consideration simultaneously several variables that may impact the outcome of the measurement and disease under study.

Mutagenicity: The potential for adverse changes in the genetic make-up of an organism, that is, mutations.

Multiple source product: A product with at least one other product that is generically equivalent, therapeutically equivalent, or pharmaceutically equivalent, as determined by the FDA approvals and a health system's pharmacy and therapeutics committee or equivalent.

Mutual recognition procedure: A process for product approvals where a centralized assessment and approval process is performed on behalf of and agreed upon in advance for several countries, states, or health systems.

N

Nanoparticles: Particles that possess a very small size of 100 millionths of a millimeter (1-100 nm).

Nanotechnology: Use of nanoparticle size in research and product development to achieve new functionality of a product, such as better tissue penetration or distribution, for example, pegylation and liposomes product development.

National accounts manager (NAM): A sales person in a management position that particularly deals with large customers or customer groups, for example, a hospital group or a national managed care organization, including selling the company's product creating a contract for the group, assessing the customer's business and possible relationships with the company, and serving as the liaison to the company.

National drug code (NDC): A numbering system in the United States for all drug products where each product is given an individual number (11 digits) that indicates the labeler company, product, and package size.

National health expenditures (NHE): All the payments and costs for direct and indirect costs related to drug products, devices, and services in the delivery of health care for all diseases by a nation.

National Institutes of Health (NIH): The medical and scientific research division of the U.S. federal government with separate disease oriented research divisions involved in basic, translational, clinical, and systems research. Work is done in their own laboratories, through funded research at universities and research institutions, and in collaboration with the industry.

National practitioner (provider) identifier: A ten digit number given by the Centers for Medicare and Medicaid Services, unique to each healthcare provider, for any claims related to healthcare activities for Medicare or Medicaid.

Net present value (NPV): The projection of the financial worth of a product in dollars, taking into consideration all costs for research, development, marketing and manufacturing, success probabilities at each major development stage, and the forecast of sales for the marketing lifetime of the product.

Net sales: Gross sales revenue less cash discounts and all other price reductions that reduce the amount paid to the manufacturer.

New business development (NBD): A marketing group at a biopharma company that deals with pipeline products and supports the research and development division, as well as reporting to senior management, their market information, market research, and anlayses, including sales potential, sales forecasts, early marketing and education programs, customer/provider feedback on market potential, and optimal product profiles for diseases.

New Drug Application/Biologic License Application (NDA/BLA): The comprehensive set of documents for an investigational product provided to the FDA that document the efficacy, safety, and quality of a product in applying for marketing authorization. The documents include administrative information, chemistry, manufacturing, and controls, non-clinical pharmacology and toxicology, human pharmacokinetics and bioavailability, formulation information, microbiology (for an anti-infective), clinical data with statistics (protocols, study reports, data tables, informed consent, and case report forms for all phases—I, II, and III), publications, pediatric use information, as applicable, samples, labeling, and packaging, patent information and certification, and financial certifications or disclosures.

New molecular entity (NME): An active ingredient that has never been marketed in this country and is novel in regard to its structure, mechanism of action, or indication.

Niche market: A specific disease or indication for a product that is relatively narrow in scope, commensurately smaller in size, that is, number of patients and possibly sales potential, as well as used usually by medical specialists.

NIH Roadmap: A research initiative led by the National Institutes of Health to support companies and universities with tools to assist in discovery and facilitate development of hits and leads in emerging high risk areas of science. A center has been created in New Mexico, the Molecular Libraries Screening Center, for high-throughput assays of prospective targets and making the information available on-line. Another center, the Chemical Genomics Center, has been created for genomics screening.

Nominal price: A price that is less than 10% of the average manufacturer's price.

Non-Inferiority trial: A study that tries to show that one drug is similarly effective to a standard drug, and hence proving the null hypothesis correct (no difference). You can only say that one drug is not better than the other. It is also called an "equivalence" trial. It uses an "active" comparator. It is increasingly used due to concerns regarding placebo-controlled trials. Non-inferiority cannot be taken alone as evidence of efficacy in NDA/BLA applications with the FDA in U.S.

Normal saline (NS): A solution of 0.9% sodium chloride in water.

Not approvable letter: Written communication from the FDA to a sponsor that applied for marketing authorization that designates the application as not approvable based on deficiencies in the application, that is, low benefit-risk ratio, inadequate demonstration of efficacy or safety.

Notice of inspection (NOI): An FDA letter that indicates an inspection will be done at a company.

Novelty: For a product patent, it must be reasonably unique and different from the "prior art." The invention must not be known or previously published in the art.

Number needed to treat (NNT): A statistical calculation of the number of patients that need to be treated in a study to achieve a proposed outcome or change in a disease parameter, as well as achieve a specific level of power (reasonable level of statistical certainty that an outcome was real and not by chance).

O

Obviousness: In patenting a product, the inventor can not simply take "the next obvious step" in the science. The scientific advance must be reasonably significant.

Office of Inspector General (OIG): The area in the Justice Department of the U.S. government that oversees that proper business practices are being used by the pharmaceutical industry in its dealings with the government and public, in accordance with laws and regulations. They can investigate, accuse, and take a company to court, including the potential for legal penalties, such as jail time or financial awards to the government or injured parties.

Off-label: Use of a product not included in the approved product labeling (non-approved indication).

Oligonucleotide: A biologic molecule comprised of nucleic acids whose size (length of the chain) is small to modest, for example, 25–50 nucleic acids; most often a small RNA molecule.

On-label: Use of a product for an indication that is approved by a regulatory authority.

Open formulary: List of drugs to be used for patients in a healthcare system, permitting any drug approved for use to be prescribed.

Operating committee (OC): The senior executive team at a company usually comprised of at least the CEO, COO, CMO, CFO, and CIO, responsible for strategy, and plans, decisions, and operations for financial, personnel, product matters.

Operating costs: All the costs to run a department or operation that excludes staff and equipment.

Opinion-leader (OL): Influencer on current medical practice, research, or education, who is capable of inspiring peers to improve patient outcomes through their research excellence, scientific literature credentials, or clinical expertise, and has an esteemed position at a prominent institution of work.

Opportunity analysis: Market research that examines the potential or future benefits of a molecule or product to a company, such as compound ratings, product profile for a minimum versus desirable profile along with sales forecast, bubble diagrams for efficacy versus safety with market size, and new molecular entities versus mechanisms of action.

Options, stock: Stock shares awarded to employees as a bonus that carry a certain value on the day of the award, but need to be purchased by the employee at some point in the future usually within a specified time period.

Orange book: A U. S. government created book containing the list of FDA-approved drug products with therapeutic evaluations, especially for generically equivalent products.

Orphan drugs: FDA program to promote the development of products that demonstrate promise for the diagnosis and/or treatment of a rare disease, as defined as prevalence in United States of less than 200,000 cases.

Outcomes research: A more global evaluation of the value of a product to a healthcare system or disease, including efficacy, toxicity and cost factors, usually in practical patient populations and healthcare settings. Types of data and studies may include pharmacoeconomics, such as, cost-benefit, cost-utility, cost-effectiveness, and cost-minimization; productivity; days of work lost; quality-of-life/outcomes; patient preferences; willingness-to-pay; and drug or morbidity utilization evaluation.

Out-of-pocket (OOP): Expenses (payments) by patients outside of Medicare or private insurance coverage for healthcare costs.

Out-licensing: Process for a product being sold to another company, usually including marketing, research, and patent rights.

Out-sourcing: A company that possesses products, but may have less than all the needed staff, can use service companies, outside of and separate from the company, that can perform various activities, rather than adding full-time staff, for example, clinical research, market research, regulatory affairs, biostatistics, and drug distribution.

Overall response rate (ORR): The global change in a disease that takes into consideration all the key monitoring parameters for a disease.

Over-the-counter (OTC) drug: Non-prescription drug item.

P

P's (4) of marketing: Product, Price, Place, and Promotion

Package insert (PI): The product information approved by the FDA and accompanying the product with its packaging (pharmacology, clinical data, indications and usage, dose, contraindications, warnings and precautions, adverse reactions, drug abuse and dependence, overdosage, formulation, administration, how supplied). Intended end-users are physicians, pharmacists, and nurses. Package insert drives number and type of clinical trials required to establish efficacy and safety. Negotiation of labeling language is one of the last tasks of a new drug application submission review. This language is used as the basis in advertising copy.

Packaging: The container system and accompanying labeling for a product, such as a vial and box for an injectable or inhaled product. It can be associated with delivery of products, for example, prefilled syringe, metered dose inhaler, or single unit dosing. Patient needs must be considered, for example, multiple dose versus unit dose packaging, vials versus prefilled syringes. Outpatient products must be child resistant. Package should be tamper evident. Novel technologies are being investigated to prevent counterfeiting (e.g., radio frequency identification). Packaging ensures that the product is as stable as feasible during normal storage conditions. Protection from contamination, moisture, and light may be required. Low cost of goods is important for profitability and market competitiveness.

Parallel tract program: An accelerated regulatory pathway for a new drug application leading to marketing approval, wherein several studies or projects normally done sequentially are done in parallel, for example, metabolism studies, phase 2 studies, and mutagenicity laboratory research.

Particulates: Visible contaminants in the liquid formulation of a product, which can be, for example, impurities, microbial contaminants, or product aggregation.

Patent: For a new subject material, device, or manufacturing process, recognition (documentation) of legal protection from copying or duplication for the item is awarded by the patent office, for which the five standard parameters have been established: composition of matter, non-obviousness, disclosure, novelty, and utility.

Patent term restoration: The federal action that affords an innovator product a patent extension for being first to market among competitive products, along with expedited generic drug approvals. Marketing exclusivity periods are 7 years for orphan drugs, 5 years for innovator products, 3 years for selected changes in an approved drug product, and 6 months for pediatric studies and labeling completed.

Patent certification: In an NDA/BLA, a company must document for the FDA that it has a current and enforceable patent.

Patient package insert (PPI): The product information designed for the patient to guide in its use and the understanding of the product's use, benefits, and risks. It accompanies the product, provided in the box or by the pharmacist.

Patient selection: For clinical studies, patients need to be chosen, which involves a variety of key elements, that is, their identification, screening, qualifying (per inclusion and exclusion study criteria), agreeability to participate, and enrolling, that is, consenting, interviewing (with data recording in case report forms), and baseline testing (per study lab or other tests).

Payer: Individual, group or company that pays for products or services. Payers include patients and their family, health insurance companies, managed care organizations, employers, and state and federal government agencies.

Payment for participation: It is in accord with the traditions and ethics of society to pay people who participate and cooperate in activities that benefit others, which may also include clinical studies. The institutional review board should review any proposed remuneration. Remuneration should not be beyond a token gesture for participation, and is best if discussed before the study's initiation. Serious ethical questions exist when payment is made to adults who are acting on behalf of minors in return for allowing minors to participate as research subjects. Waiver of medical costs may be permitted.

Peak plasma concentration: The highest concentration of a drug in the plasma following a single dose.

Pediatric exclusivity: A manufacturer can receive patent extension of six months extending the exclusive marketing of their product, if they successfully pursue an amendment in their new drug application for a pediatric labeling and use.

Pediatric investigational plan (PIP): An agreement for specifically designated research in pediatric areas for a product between the FDA and the manufacturer to pursue pediatric labeling. The product can be under an investigative new drug or can be a new drug application-approved product.

Pediatric Research Equity Act (PREA): Law in 2003 that requires pediatric studies to be done for all new drugs and labeling for new indications, dosage forms, dosing regimens, route of administration, and ingredients. The Pediatric Advisory Committee is created at the FDA. Waivers are permitted where pediatric use is not likely or the product is life-saving, and the FDA does not want to hold up approval process. Orphan drugs are exempt.

Pediatric use information: Safety and effectiveness, including appropriate dosing, administration, and formulation, for claimed indications in all relevant pediatric populations.

Pegylation: Attachment of polyethylene glycol molecule to a drug or biological product to alter its pharmacokinetics usually extending its half-life and stretching the dosing frequency. For example, interferon is given three times per week versus peg-interferon is given weekly.

PeriApproval: Around the time of product approval (usually 1-2 years before and 1-2 years after the regulatory approval).

Periodic adverse experience report (PAER): After a product's approval by the FDA in the United States, adverse events must be recorded, categorized, tabulated, and then submitted to the FDA periodically. It is a quarterly requirement initially and then annually for the commercial life of the product, according to the approval requirements.

Permeability: A property of a product that indicates its ability to penetrate across or through biologic membranes.

Personalized medicine: The use of genomic data with patients that identifies differences in patients' drug response profiles (efficacy, safety, and/or pharmacokinetics) and predicts the best possible treatment options.

PG signature: Genomic make-up of a patient for a particular trait(s).

Pharmaceutical assistance program (PAP): Marketed product is provided by a pharmaceutical company to patients at a reduced price or for free, usually based on financial need of the patient, which is often below the federal poverty level, or with the addition of health care and other expenses, well in excess of all income sources.

Pharmaceutical equivalents: FDA considers drug products to be pharmaceutical equivalents if they meet these three criteria: they contain the same active ingredient(s); they are of the same dosage form and route of administration; and they are identical in strength or concentration. Pharmaceutically equivalent drug products may differ in characteristics such as shape, release mechanism, labeling (to some extent), scoring, and excipients (including colors, flavors, and preservatives).

Pharmaceutical Executive: Journal about and for the pharmaceutical industry addressing industry and management issues, from research to marketing.

Pharmaceutical pricing agreement: This agreement is required for manufacturers who have executed a Medicaid Rebate Agreement with CMS and voluntary for those who do not have a current Medicaid Rebate Agreement. The pharmaceutical pricing agreement must be signed by a corporate officer of the company (e.g., President, Chief Executive Officer, or General Counsel—signatures by VP or Director of Sales or Marketing will not be accepted). A pharmaceutical pricing agreement remains in effect until terminated by either the manufacturer or the secretary of Health and Human Services. It is not automatically terminated if a manufacturer terminates its Medicaid Rebate Agreement.

Pharmaceutics (PHC): The scientific discipline that creates formulations for products and studies their physical and chemical properties, pharmacokinetic parameters, and stability.

Pharmacodynamics (PD): The effects of a drug on the body (the pharmacology and toxicology), especially the impact on disease or disease markers, as well as timecourse for these effects and their magnitude. Pharmacokinetic requirements may also be included.

Pharmacoeconomics (PE): (1) The study of net economic impact of selection and use of pharmaceuticals on total cost of delivering health care. (2) Pharmacoeconomics employs a more global perspective and a more objective balance of benefits and costs. (3) Health care utilization (efficiency) with a focus on "value" is another definition. (4) Furthermore, it can be defined as a benefit for money spent.

Pharmacoepidemiology: Observational studies regarding drug usage in representative disease populations of the real world. They are characterized by large size, prospective or retrospective, longitudinal over a specified time, well-defined hard endpoint, and the use of comparator control groups (matched controls based on disease or drug use). Information sources include databases, patient registries, and charts/medical histories. Goals for the target disease may include identification and characterization of product usage (drug choices, uses, dosing, adverse events, or types of prescribers) over a time period, along with disease descriptors and/or practice patterns. Cohort design involves a group of patients with exposure to specific products or a specific disease. Case control design involves a collection of individual cases of patients with a specific exposure or reaction and matched controls from same population.

Pharmacogenomic (PG): Study of genes and gene fragments for their impact on drug actions that differentiate patients in normal health and for their relationship to disease progression and mitigation.

Pharmacokinetics (PK): The study of the absorption, distribution, blood and tissue levels, metabolism, and elimination of drugs, biologicals, and chemicals, including the specific mechanisms, mathematical calculations, and impact on drug and patient outcomes.

Pharmacology: Mechanisms of action, effects of drugs on animals or patients, and pharmacokinetic studies.

Pharmacophore: A specific structural construct of a drug or molecule, including its stereochemistry and electronic charge, that will interact with a specific receptor to produce a biological action.

Pharmacotherapy (PT): The use of drugs and biologicals to mitigate disease pathology and/or its signs and symptoms.

Pharmacovigilance (PV): The systems and processes to identify, evaluate, and report adverse events with a company's products.

Pharmacy and therapeutics committee (P&T): A group of healthcare professionals at an institution responsible for drug policies and selection of products available for use, based on safety, efficacy, and cost, as well as any unique characteristics of the institution and their patient population.

Pharmacy benefits management (PBM): A private company, outside of the government and separate from the manufacturer, that contracts with employers, provider groups, or healthcare institutions that care for patients, focusing on product usage. They monitor and help control usage of prescription products, intending to lower overall drug costs while maintaining quality health care, for which they receive a fee for their services. Formularies, treatment guidelines, and generic product substitution are three approaches commonly used by pharmacy benefits managements.

Phase 0 study: Earliest study in humans at micro-doses to determine early safety and pharmacokinetic information. In 2006, this type of study was an FDA initiative to accelerate product development.

Phase 1 study: First studies in humans after obtaining an investigative new drug application. Single-doses are used. Work is followed by short-term, multiple dose studies with follow-up for days to weeks. Goals are to determine initial safety profile, maximally tolerated dose (MTD), and pharmacokinetic profile including absorption, distribution, metabolism, and excretion. Usually 20–100 healthy volunteers are involved. For studies of "toxic" therapies (e.g., oncology, AIDS studies), "volunteers" will have target disease for the product. Duration of all the work is generally about 1.5 years.

Phase 2 study: Clinical study in patients with target disease to establish proof of principle that the product actually possesses activity, along with safety continuing to be examined in patients. Objectives include determination of an appropriate dose (dose-ranging studies) and identification of the side effects/toxicity profile (usually over 4–6 weeks of product use). Typically 100–300 patient volunteers are involved. Overall duration of all such studies collectively is about 2 years. Post-approval phase 2 work identifies and tests potential new uses (e.g., areas of unmet medical need), examines different dosing regimens and routes of administration, and assesses its role with concomitant disease/drugs and effects in special populations.

Phase 2a study: Early study in patients with target disease for safety and some desirable drug effect.

Phase 2b study: Later phase 2 study in patients with target disease with dosing determination, establishment of proof of principle, and some examination of efficacy. Alternative strategy is to explore efficacy at multiple doses in a large trial or multifactorial design and request pivotal trial consideration.

Phase 3 study: These larger studies confirm effectiveness in the target disease and the more complete side effect profile. They form the primary basis to establish efficacy for product approval ("pivotal studies"). They must be adequate and well-controlled studies. Typically two positive, well-designed studies are required. Adverse events are monitored over a longer period (12–24 weeks). Design of study creates the primary framework for the package insert and for marketing the product. Usually 1,000–3,000 patient volunteers are involved at many sites with many investigators. Overall duration for all studies is about 2.5 years, unless long-term studies or mortality endpoints are needed over a multi-year period. The FDA often prefers placebo comparisons whereas the rest of the world usually employs active comparators, as long as a standard of care exists. In some countries activity versus comparator influences initial price allowance.

Phase 3b trial: Studies performed during the time period between completion of phase 3 studies and marketing approval (as much as 2–3 years). Goals may include an expanded adverse event database, more dosing and efficacy data before approval, increased familiarity among more physicians (e.g., those in practice-based settings) and institutions, and additional publications. Often, they are large in size and may include sub-studies in certain populations. Their design requires FDA approval, and the trials are filed under the investigational new drug application.

Phase 4 study: Clinical study at this stage occur after product approval for marketing. They are often very large studies with a simpler design; however, institutional review board approvals are needed. The FDA often requires them as part of the marketing approval, and failure to fulfill FDA requirements can result in withdrawal of approval. With growing safety concerns, trends are toward regular FDA requirement today. Objectives may include comparison to competitor drugs, use to define mechanisms of disease (often investigator-initiated), identifying subpopulations, evaluating new dosing schema, exploring "real-world" effectiveness (e.g., in the office practice with very typical patients), examining impact of concurrent diseases, post-marketing surveillance, and studying drug interactions.

Pipeline: Products in research at a company (discovery, basic research, clinical research, and marketed products for new indications).

Pivotal clinical trial: A phase 3 study, which is adequate and well-controlled, intended to establish a product's efficacy and safety for approvability of a product.

Place: The marketing principle for products that takes into consideration the channel, distribution scheme, patient flow, setting (office vs. hospital), formularies, product support, access to products for patients programs and for market research.

Placebo control: A treatment group in a study design wherein no active substance is contained in the formulation being used in order to compare a potentially active product to no treatment.

Planning cycle: The eight steps for the creation and implementation of plans, in following order: planning, concept, design, plan, allocate, execute, deliver, review, and support.

Planning, operational: In a plan, generally refers to the process of aligning specific goals and objectives with the activities, time-frames, resources, and responsibilities necessary for execution. It tends to be short- to intermediate-term.

Planning, strategic: The rationale and overarching ideas, as well as needs, in the plans for a product portfolio, such as its research, manufacturing, promotion, or other major functions.

Planning, tactical: The specific activities in a marketing or research plan for each goal or objective to be done to support a product.

Plan of action (POA): The regular and periodic marketing plans for selling and supporting (promotion) of a product to health professionals, payers, or patients, including educational and promotional efforts, as well as clinical trials.

Platform: In discovery (basic research), a technology for identifying, validating, or characterizing molecules or product candidates, such as monoclonal antibodies, x-ray crystallography, polymerase chain reaction, RNA blockade, and informatics.

Podium policy: FDA speeches in public forums that outline the very latest thinking about regulations, research requirements, and possible guidelines.

Points to Consider: From the FDA, these are written guidelines with recommendations for designing or conducting clinical trials in specific therapeutic areas or for specific types of designs, but they are not requirements.

Polymorphism: A single mutation in a gene at one nucleotide locus that potentially changes gene expression with a modified protein that may possess different properties, for example, the activity of an enzyme with a drug.

Portfolio of products: List of different products that a company possesses usually categorized into pharmacologic or therapeutic areas, medical practice groups, diseases, or business units.

Portfolio management (PM): Coordination, communications, and leadership of the planning, timing, responsibilities, budgeting, and especially prioritization for all the molecules in the research and development efforts at a company. Pipeline gaps in terms of timing of new products availability or missing products may be resolved through in-licensing products or technology at various stages of development.

Positioning: A marketing term that suggests how a product will be used in clinical practice or how it will be presented in promotional materials by the company, that is, its "position."

Post-approval commitments or Post-marketing commitments (PAC, PMC): A study required by the FDA to be done by the sponsor after approval, as a condition for the approval process, and product marketing. Clinical work may include safety data in additional patients, long-term safety data, special patient populations (i.e., renal failure, diabetes, geriatrics, or pediatrics), and drug interactions studies. Chemistry, manufacturing, and controls may be involved such as long-term stability, further manufacturing data at scale. Certain educational requirements may need to be done.

Post-marketing report: Submission of reports to the FDA after the approval of a new drug application for a product, especially including adverse reaction reports (15-day alerts, periodic adverse drug event reports), as well as annual reports.

Post-marketing surveillance (PMS): The various studies and research performed to evaluate a product after it has been approved for use and marketed, particularly for adverse events.

Post-translational modification: The production of proteins by mammalian cells includes alteration of the molecule after translation (RNA code to protein), such as glycosylation, sulfation, methylation, or phosphorylation, disulfide bridging, helical loops of domains, and 3-dimensional configuration, which may be required for full activity of the molecule.

Potency: Amount by weight or units of a product to produce an effect. Potency equals activity divided by mass of a drug.

Pre-approval inspections (PAI): A visit to a sponsor of a new drug application by a regulatory authority as part of the approval process for marketing, especially to assess good manufacturing practices and good clinical practices. For manufacturing and testing facilities, pre-approval inspections verify documentation in marketing application, ensure material is produced in compliance with good manufacturing practices, and ensure validation of equipment, manufacturing and control processes, and test procedures. For the clinical research, any records may be examined or any staff member may be interviewed to assess good clinical practices and adequate documentation.

Pre-clinical research: Studies in animals or in vitro (e.g., pharmacology, toxicology, pharmacokinetics, formulations, or stability) prior to human studies.

Preferred provider organization (PPO): A group of providers responsible for the delivery of health care directly to a group of patients and contract with payers at a reduced compensation rate, but as a preferred healthcare provider for that health system, employer, insurance company, or other payer.

Premarketing risk assessment: The measures regarding adverse event evaluation and follow-up recommended by the regulatory authorities such as the FDA in guidance for a company to perform throughout all stages of a product's clinical development in studies and with investigators.

Premium: Gift to a customer, for example, a book, pen, globe, or trip, as part of product promotion. Education and patient care benefits are the primary requirements for use of the premiums, according to best marketing practices suggested by the Pharmaceutical Research and Manufacturers Association.

Prescription benefits management (PBM): A function by a healthcare company in which they process prescriptions for filling, along with several oversight roles, for example, appropriateness of product selection, possible generic substitution, and patient counseling for compliance. The goals are to offer a higher level of cost-effective patient care to a payer or employer for their enrollees or employees.

Prescription drug advertising: All the promotional activity from a sponsor to the intended target audiences who will use its products, that is, all written and broadcast ads to both prescribers and consumers, and verbal exchanges between prescribers and pharmaceutical sales representatives. Only approved labeling may be used in such promotional communications (advertising). Claims made by a sponsor that are not supported by FDA-approved labeling result in misbranding. Fair balance of information is examined as well. Advertising regulations do not apply to non-promotional and independent scientific and educational exchanges.

Prescription drug advisory committee: The multidisciplinary group of experts for a therapeutic area or drug group that is chosen and convened by the FDA to offer advice about the approvability of new products.

Prescription drug-to-OTC switch: A change that permits OTC (over-the-counter) marketing of a product that was once available only by prescription. It requires approval by the FDA, and it can be done as long as a patient can safely select and consume the product without healthcare professional initiation. It occurs generally after petition by the sponsor and the collection and analysis of in-market safety data.

Prescription drug card: A card provided to patients by government or healthcare systems for drug purchases by prescription within a specific healthcare plan, usually through a health insurance company, managed care organization, prescription benefits company, or government agency.

Prescription drug plan (PDP): In the Medicare drug program, a retail pharmacy provider entity, health system, prescription benefits management company, or equivalent heathcare service entity creates a plan to provide prescription drugs and related services to a specified segment of Centers for Medicare and Medicaid Services beneficiaries for a contracted fee to be paid by Medicare.

Prevalence: The number of people alive on a certain date who have been diagnosed with a specific disease at any time in their lives. This differs from incidence in that it considers both newly diagnosed and previously diagnosed people.

Price: The amount of money charged for a product based on the value proposition, which usually also takes into consideration reimbursement opportunity and mechanisms, discounts, competitive products, rebates to healthcare systems, and the economics of the target disease in question. In some countries, the pharmacologic activity of a compound relative to a market standard influences the allowable price.

Price capping: Generally an upper price limit usually imposed by a drug sponsor on expensive products with variable doses and schedules, even if the cost for the total doses goes above the fixed amount (cap).

PRICE (performance management model): Pinpoint (key things with most impact), Record (present level of performance), Involve (bring everyone who can impact area and ask them how to improve), Coach, and Evaluate.

Pricing committee: (1) In many European and Asian countries, an official government group is charged with the responsibility to weigh the cost of a product and its clinical merit in comparison to existing treatments and decide if the government will pay for the product at all or select a price that it will pay in negotiation with the manufacturer. (2) This may also refer to a manufacturer's internal committee charged with the responsibility of price setting.

Pricing decision: Determination of the price of the product is a process that should answer a set of questions to guide the decision. Are you setting a price or establishing value? Has a thorough competitive analysis been done? Do you understand all aspects of reimbursement (public, private and disease)? Can you create value through better outcomes and/or better formulations? What data do you have and will you need (clinical, vis-vis, efficacy, novelty, safety, convenience, and marketing)? What about second indications in other diseases? Has the international component been considered? Are there contracting and distribution policies to factor in? Have you considered both long- and short-term issues? Do you understand the impact of price on your customers (providers, payers, patients, and policy-makers)?

Primary care provider (PCP): A healthcare person, usually involved in family medicine, general practice, or internal medicine, who administers broad-based medical care for patients, making referrals to specialists as needed.

Principal investigator (PI): The lead scientist responsible for conduct of a study, including ensuring safety of participants (patients or volunteers), conduct of all staff at the investigative site, and compliance with the protocol, the budget, and good clinical practices. Co-investigator(s) assist the principal investigator. Both principal and co-investigators are listed on FDA Form 1572.

Priority review: A faster FDA review time, usually within six months of new drug application/biologics license application submission, based on the product's potential for significant improvements in efficacy and/or safety, compared to marketed products.

Probability: The chance that an event occurs. It is usually expressed as a percent. Zero percent denotes impossibility, whereas 100% denotes certainty.

Probability of phase transition: The likelihood that an investigational new product will successfully move from one research phase to the next one.

Probability of success: A statistical calculation of the likelihood that a program, project, or study will result in a desired and specified positive outcome.

Probe: A tool in research that may be a protein or nucleic acid molecule that is used to find or identify a matching molecule by its structure and or function.

Process analytical technology: A system for design, analysis, and control of manufacturing with the goal of ensuring product quality, involving quality and performance attributes measured periodically during the process for raw and in-process materials and processes.

Process engineering: Goal of manufacturing is to provide a pure, stable, and safe product at high yield, reproducibly and cost-effectively, which also is the overall goal of the group called process engineering. They focus on process improvements. Examples follow. Equipment and processing schemes will likely vary depending on batch size. Purity of active ingredients must be defined and used to establish its safety and efficacy at all stages of product evolution, as in animal safety, human clinical trials, and commercial manufacturing. Critical manufacturing parameters, for example, temperature, raw material concentrations, and solvents, which can affect the purity, efficacy, and quality of both active ingredients and final products, must be established early and modified throughout development.

Process maps: Details of a process or program, for example, a clinical study conducted by a company, usually in a flow diagram for all the key steps in the process from the start to finish.

Process validation: The review and documentation by experts for the function or process (a set of procedures, systems, equipment, and staffing) that performs a function is an acceptable, reliable, and reproducible, manner and is likely to achieve successful outcomes as intended.

Prodrug: A drug substance that is marketed and consumed by patients that undergoes a chemical change in and by the human body to an active molecule (usually as a result of metabolism).

Product: (1) A marketed molecule for a therapeutic use. (2) The drug or biological molecule also can be considered to include the label, its positioning, the packaging, unmet medical need being met, and the manufacturing process.

Product candidate: A drug or biological product that has advanced through research and pre-clinical development successfully and moves on to become a potential marketable, safe and effective product, but it is still in clinical research.

Product complaint: Communication to a manufacturer regarding a problem with a final product, for example, formulation or container system, any packaging issue, or even labeling, but not an adverse event or efficacy question.

Product development: (1) Research strategy, plans, processes, staffing, resources, and outcomes for the clinical studies program for a product. (2) Also, the division at a company responsible for the previously mentioned items for all pipeline products.

Product plan: The major events and timeframes for a product's life cycle from research to post-marketing, including clinical development strategy, market development, clinical operations, safety issues, manufacturing, and regulatory strategy and milestones.

Product profile: Description of key properties of the product, which can be used by the research and development team and the sales and marketing team to develop the studies and research plan, such as efficacy, safety, formulation, pharmacokinetics, dosing and administration, patent status, and manufacturing. It often contains comparative information for product competitors.

Product quality defects: Risks with drug products based on problems with manufacturing, packaging, and their labeling.

Professional services: The department in a company responsible usually for customer interactions and internal technical support, including medical information (on-label and off-label issues), triage of customer inquiries (public, patients, providers, payers, investors, and press), medical education, marketing support (technical input and oversight), sales training (technical and clinical), medical science liaisons, and phase 4 clinical research. It is also called Medical Affairs at many companies.

Profitability: (1) A measure of a company's ability to make money. (2) It is the net financial value of a company, that is, sales, income, assets, and productivity, minus costs including all staffing, expenses, and losses.

Profit margin: Usually expressed as a percentage of profit divided by revenue. It is net profit before taxes minus cost of goods sold and operating expenses.

Project management: Management and coordination, possibly leadership, of a team of cross-department people responsible for progress of molecules as they advance from research to launch and beyond, including budget, staffing, and deadlines. Key elements include coordination of project components; communication within the team, out of the team, and to upper management; and assisting in decision-making.

Project management team: Project team typically includes variety of functional groups with responsibilities for development plan and conduct of clinical trials: project management, clinical research, regulatory, pharmacology and toxicology, chemistry, pharmaceutics, manufacturing, safety group, marketing, biostatistics, and data management.

Promotion: Activities by marketing and sales people in the process of demand generation for a product with the targeted customers using advertising or educational materials after the product's approval for marketing. Elements also include media advertising, publications, public relations, and direct-to-consumer advertising.

Prompt pay discounts: Any discount off the purchase price routinely paid by a manufacturer to a wholesaler or to a retailer, if the product is received directly from the manufacturer, for payment for products within a specified time limit usually specified by the contract or invoice.

Proof-of-concept (POC): An animal study, usually, that establishes a desirable drug action that is being sought by a researcher. Also, a phase 2 study in humans that establishes drug action in a target disease.

Proof-of-principal (POP): An animal study, usually, that establishes a desirable drug action that is being sought by a researcher. Also, a phase 2 study in humans that establishes drug action in a target disease.

Proprietary interest: Property or any financial interest in a product or company, including, but not limited to, a patent, trademark, copyright, licensing agreement, or stock.

Protein: A sequence of amino acids of varying lengths, usually over 50–100 amino acids, along with its tertiary structures, such as glycosylation, peptide domains, and three-dimensional folding, that possesses a physiologic or pharmacologic activity in animals or plants.

Proteome: The complete listing and description of all the proteins and their functions for an organism.

Protocol: The detailed written description of a clinical trial, including key background information about the disease and its therapy, study objectives, patient selection criteria, design parameters (control groups), treatments, methods, and procedures for monitoring patients, safety considerations, and statistical methods that will be used to analyze data.

Protocol amendments: Changes in the design of a study that must be formally written out and approved by an institutional review board.

Provider: Physician, pharmacist, nurse, physical therapist, or other care giver for patients.

Public health advisory: An FDA communication to the general population, healthcare professionals, and manufacturers related to serious adverse effects with drugs and the need to take specific actions as recommended to reduce health risks.

Publication planning: The process at a company to document in the medical literature the full value of a product undergoing investigational trials and about to be marketed, or for a marketed product to further document future therapeutic uses. Tasks include creating what key messages will be important for a product in its markets, based its key features and fit (benefits and limits); identifying what publications will be needed to be done potentially along with major study design attributes, key possible outcomes, possible authors, and journal placements; addressing the timeframes for publication of the list of publications; and assisting the research and development management to extract as much applicable data from all the studies done by the company to assist with positioning the product in the most appropriate manner for patient care and optimal product use.

Public relations (PR): The interface of the company with the general public, especially with the media, including any communications.

Purity: The property of a product that describes the lack of any contamination by an undesired material in the product and the concentration of only the desired active ingredients, expressed usually as percentage of purity.

Pyrogenicity: The property of a product wherein the extent of the potential to contain contaminants that can produce febrile reactions to the product in patients is measured in animal studies.

Q

Quality assurance (QA): Company process wherein systems, processes, procedures, staffing, and actual outcomes are assessed to maintain, correct, or improve quality.

Quality control (QC): In-process and final testing to establish and assess conformance of products and processes to predetermined specifications. Stability testing of final products is another component of quality control.

Quality adjusted life years (QALY): In quality of life studies, a determination of the number of years of extended life with added benefits to the patients from the intervention being studied.

Quality-of-life studies (QOL): Research in patients that addresses outcomes beyond standard efficacy and safety to include humanistic parameters improving the daily life of a patient. Quality-of-life studies can involve disease-specific parameters (e.g., FACT survey in cancer) versus general parameters for any disease or patient situation (e.g., SF-36 health survey).

Query: (1) A check of data, processes, or systems to assess their accuracy or completeness, especially with case report forms for clinical studies. (2) Also, it is an interaction with a regulatory authority where they are questioning the company. (3) Also, it is a question from a patient or care giver about a product.

Quid pro quo: Giving something of equal value back in a transaction.

R

Randomization code: An assignment numbering system typically prepared by biostatistics that directs investigators as to which drug treatment each subject is to receive, in a manner wherein the next recipient receives a treatment absent of any influence by anyone and any process (random).

Randomized trial: A research study wherein the assignment of subjects to treatment groups is performed eliminating bias through the use of random numbers.

Raw data: Information or statistics about the subjects or their changes during any study obtained directly from patients, providers, or medical records without any manipulation that has been recorded usually on case report forms.

Reach: The extent of exposure to promotional vehicles of various types, for example, the number of target physicians called on, or the number of healthcare professionals receiving a specific promotion. Often part of "reach and frequency" calculation.

Rebate: An amount paid back by a manufacturer to a wholesale or retail customer, as a percentage or fixed amount of the total sales, for the purchase of a certain amount of product over a particular time period.

Recall: The return of a product, usually a specific manufactured lot that, to a company because of some defect, for example, subpotency, stability, dissolution failure, label mix-up, content uniformity failure, microbial contamination, or violation of a good manufacturing practice. It can be either a voluntary or FDA required action.

Reconciliation: Resolution of an error or missing information, usually between the case report form of a patient in a study with the actual medical records.

Records retention: Timeframes, methods, and operating procedures for storage and retaining of documents.

Refuse to file: FDA refusal to allow filing of a new drug application due to a significant deficiency.

Registry, patient: A program identifying patients with a specific disease or treatment and collecting information about them, in order to identify research subjects for studies, to report adverse events, to identify indigent patients needing product support, or to collect data from traditional patients who have received a particular treatment.

Regulation: An action described by or taken by a government agency with oversight responsibility, published and formally announced, that directs specific behaviors, actions, processes, procedures, records, or outcomes to be performed by a company or individual in performance of the research or marketing of a product.

Regulatory affairs (RA): Group at a company responsible as the official interface with, and expertise concerning, government agencies that regulate and approve products and materials, and related practices such as research, marketing, or manufacturing. They are experts in the regulations and laws governing the operations of the biopharma industry. They often possess oversight of the company in compliance with these regulations and laws.

Regulatory authority: The government agency in a country responsible for approving healthcare products for marketing (drugs, biologicals, and devices), ensuring public safety in the use of healthcare products, promulgating drug use policies as it relates to safety, efficacy, and quality (manufacturing), as well as approval criteria and processes, monitoring advertising and promotion of products, and monitoring the pharmaceutical industry for compliance with all related regulations (e.g., the FDA, and EMEA).

Reimbursement: Payment to patients by payers, after they have contracted for, received, and paid for their healthcare services or products.

Relative dose intensity (RDI): The comparison of the actual versus planned doses given to a patient, including the frequency and total amount given, over a specific period of time.

Relative risk reduction (RRR): In any endeavor, be it a clinical trial or business plan, risks exist that can thwart advancement toward the goals. Risk reduction plans identify potential problems that represent risks in order to alter the conduct or timeline of the plan or program, plan for risk aversion or mitigation actions, and use them as necessary. Such risk reduction plans and activities are used to even quantify the potential relative risk reduction.

Remaining uncertainties: Risks from medicines outside of expected adverse experiences or product quality, including unexpected side effects, long-term effects, and unstudied uses and populations, usually only observed following marketing of a product to a broad patient population.

Reproductive tox: Toxicology studies for pregnancy, teratogenicity, and fertility.

Research and development division (R&D): The area of the company responsible for conducting all the basic and clinical research in animals, in vitro, and humans about its products. Usual departments may include discovery in the laboratory for targets, leads, and product candidates, metabolism and pharmacokinetics, pharmaceutics (formulations), pharmacology, toxicology, clinical research (phases 1 through 3), biostatistics and data management, quality control and assurance, and regulatory affairs.

Resource utilization committee: Group within American Medical Association dealing with Medicare programs.

Response rate (RR): The percentage of patients that receive the desired and specified beneficial outcome from a product within a certain time period.

Rest of world (ROW): The market segment usually described as outside of the United States, Canada, European Union, Japan, China, and Australia. The third world countries comprise the majority of these countries in Africa, Asia, Eastern Europe, and South America.

Retail pharmacy: Any independent, chain, mail order, pharmacy benefits management company, or other outlet that purchases or arranges purchases of drugs from manufacturers, wholesalers, or distributors, or other licensed entity and sells or provides the drugs to the general public through prescriptions.

Return goods policy: A published statement that describes the conditions under which a company will accept products returned to them from wholesalers or retailers because of specified problems, such as outdating beyond expiration date (most often), contamination, complaints with formulation (e.g., discoloration or precipitation), or unused product.

Return-on-investment (ROI): The benefits received, usually financial, to a company, institution, or individual for a specific development or commercial activity that consumes resources.

Return-on-assets: Also known as profit-to-assets indicating both profit and asset management.

Reviewable units: A predefined portion of a new drug application submitted to the FDA by a sponsor before a full application, in order to review a segment of the application and expedite the drug development process.

Revenue: Income to a company including sales, royalties, interest, and other payments, for example, milestone payments for research.

Risk, minimal: The probability and magnitude of harm or discomfort in the research are considered to be not greater than that ordinarily encountered in the daily conduct of business.

Risk management: The effort, processes, systems and people that attempt to reduce the risk of problems or delays in product development in any department. Examples of assessments include time-to-market versus risk of failure, probability of success by phase, risk scoring, and decision trees.

Risk minimization action plan: FDA guidance that addresses specific risk-related goals and objectives and suggests tools to minimize the risks of drug and biological products. The focus is adverse event prevention, reporting, and mitigation.

Risks of products: Nine standard categories are outlined in the following: product defects, known side effects (avoidable and unavoidable), unexpected side effects, long-term side effects, off-label effects, effects in unstudied populations, medication errors, device errors, and remaining uncertainties.

Rolling submissions: FDA drug/biologic approvals that allow for incremental submission of reviewable modules of NDA/BLA to reduce overall FDA review time and accelerate the approval process for significant new molecular entities.

S

Safe harbor: In contracting between customers and a company and in educational programming by a company, federal drug laws and regulations need to be followed, especially with the Food and Drug Administration Modernization Act, which creates areas for collaboration that are safe from negative legal action.

Safe Medical Devices Act: The Safe Medical Devices Act was passed in 1990, requiring nursing homes, hospitals, and other facilities that use medical devices to report to the FDA incidents that suggest that a medical device probably caused or contributed to the death, serious illness, or serious injury of a patient. Manufacturers are required to conduct post-marketing surveillance on permanently implanted devices whose failure might cause serious harm or death, and to establish methods for tracing and locating patients depending on such devices. The act authorizes FDA to order device product recalls and other actions.

Safety: Adverse event profile of a product.

Safety database: The data collected, recorded, and stored about a product and patient usage dealing with adverse events from a study or for the post-marketing period for a product.

Safety margin: The difference between drug doses for a dose that yields a desirable action with little adverse effects versus a higher dose with unacceptable adverse effects. The doses for IC50, NOAEL, and MTD for a product can give a numerical estimate of this margin of safety. Some researchers and clinicians also will call this the therapeutic window.

Safety officer: An individual at a company or regulatory agency who is responsible for safety with the use of specified products, including monitoring, writing procedures and policies, and reporting any related issues to the appropriate management and regulatory groups.

Sales aide: A promotional item that is used by a sales person to assist in the sales process, for example, product monograph, publication, video, or print ad.

Sales analyses : Analytical and quantitative examinations of performance based on various measures of product sales and marketing data, for example, revenue projections over time (usually daily, quarterly, and 5+ years), market share, prescription trends, competitive activity, and peak sales versus research and development costs.

Sales and marketing division (S&M): The area of the company responsible for the marketing, sales, and distribution of products. Representative departments include business units for target markets, such as inflammation versus cardiology, or family medicine versus specialty care areas, market research, marketing, sales departments (general field, hospital, and corporate accounts), advertising (usually through vendors), medical education (usually through independent medical communication groups), and national accounts.

Sales call: A meeting by a sales person with a customer.

Sales management organization (SMO): A company that provides management services to a pharmaceutical company for sales organizations, including but not limited to, organizational planning, compensation plans, recruiting of staff, providing sales people, managing the sales programs, and performing and monitoring sales activity.

Sales representative: A person directly involved in the selling of a product, usually to a healthcare professional.

Sarbanes-Oxley Act: A U.S. congressional act that directs businesses to report more openly about their financial processes and dealings, including reports to the public and government regulators. For example, the chief executive officer and chief financial officer must certify personally that all financial reports are valid. Procedures must be in place to receive, retain, and treat complaints regarding accounting and auditing matters and to allow confidential and anonymous submission by employees their concerns about these issues. Criminal and civil penalties are outlined for noncompliance or failures in action (or inaction).

Scale-up: Changes in batch size in manufacturing of the active pharmaceutical ingredient or final drug product. Product quantity increases from use for early preclinical research needs to clinical studies, and then to full market needs post approval, often require significant processing and formulation changes. Examples include required higher speeds or larger processing equipment and tanks that can alter critical parameters, such as heat distribution, mixing characteristics, and time that affect purity of material. Excipients and formulation may be modified to improve processing characteristics, such as flow of powder for compressing tablets, coating, or drying. Chemical reactions may be altered because larger volumes of liquids often take longer to obtain processing temperatures. Longer processing times can cause degradation of unstable materials, and can increase potential for bacterial growth in liquid materials.

Selling, general, and administrative costs (SG&A): All expenses incurred by a company that are not related to research and development and manufacturing costs.

Seizures: The FDA initiates an action to take possession of goods (the product) through U.S. marshals due to violation of the law.

Serious adverse event (SAE): A drug reaction that causes hospitalization or its prolongation, death, persistent disability, birth defect, cancer, a life threatening event, or an overdose.

Service fee: Any fees paid by a manufacturer to an entity that represent fair market value, for an itemized service actually performed on behalf of the manufacturer that the manufacturer would have to provide in the absence of the arrangement.

Shape the market: All the marketing activities done in advance of product approval, including the market research, product research, education, and promotion by a company, intended to focus the public and provider communities on the target areas for a future product's use.

Shape the product: All the marketing activities performed prior to product approval, including the market research, product research, education, and promotion by a company, intended to focus the public and provider communities on a future product's use, especially benefits, and limits.

Shareholder: A person who has purchased and owns stock shares in a company.

Share-of-market: The percentage of a market (product usage or sales) in a pharmacologic or therapeutic area that one product possesses in comparison to total sales.

Share-of-voice: The percentage of advertising and educational activities in a disease or therapeutic area that one product possesses in comparison to competitive products.

Shelf Keeping Unit: Area for a product on the shelf of a pharmacy.

Short-form 36: A generally applicable quality of life assessment tool with 36 questions for medical outcomes studies; 8 subscales and 2 indices (physical and mental components).

Signal: A repeated occurrence of an adverse event suggesting a rare event being detected usually at an early stage of product development, or a biological marker that can occur early and repeatedly in the course of a disease and suggests a product action, such as toxicity, efficacy, or pharmacogenomic change.

Significant payments: Any payment to an investigator or institution by a sponsor of a study to support activities of the investigator that exceed $25,000, exclusive of the costs to conduct the study (e.g., honoraria, equipment, retainers, and ongoing research). The level is used in judging conflict of interest questions.

Site: Healthcare institution or office where a study is being performed.

Site visit: Travel to a location by a sponsor or the sponsor's agent (e.g., CRO) where a study is being done for the purpose of monitoring the study conduct and compliance with protocols and procedures.

Six sigma quality: Processes and systems in any industry to ascertain and improve the quality to the highest level of the targeted group or process at a company.

Skilled nursing facility (SNF): A facility that primarily provides inpatient skilled (higher level) nursing care and related services to patients who require medical, nursing, or rehabilitative services, but it does not provide the level of care or treatment available in a hospital.

Slim jim: A sales aide or promotional piece used by a sales person that is small enough in size to fit in a pocket and that usually includes the features and benefits of a product.

Small molecule: Usually refers to a drug that impacts a target for a disease.

Small volume parenteral (SVP): An injectable product that is small in measured volume, such as those prepared in syringes, vials, or solutions of smaller sizes, often for IV admixture.

Solubility: The property of a product that refers to the quantity of it (usually maximum) that can be dissolved in a specific amount of liquid.

Source data or documents: Any information or forms from the original patient records, including any patient or family histories, clinical observations, laboratory or special tests, chart notes, dispensing or administration records, or possibly financial information in written, film or other recorded formats, that are used and collected for case report forms for a clinical trial.

Special protocol assessment (SPA): A request from the sponsor of a clinical trial for feedback from the FDA that allows a company to receive official evaluation and guidance on the design and sample size of pivotal clinical trial protocols, based on scientific intent of the investigators and sponsors. A company can request this formal assessment for a pivotal trial that is intended to form the primary basis of an efficacy claim in a new drug application. The FDA agrees to a study design for efficacy before initiation of phase 3 trial and is generally bound by this decision when the study is submitted in the NDA.

Specimen: (1) A sample amount of a product from a manufacturing lot or a tissue. (2) A fluid sample from a patient.

Sponsor: (1) A company or group that is supporting (financially) and takes responsibility for a project or study. (2) The applicant for a new drug application/common technical document.

Spontaneous report: A report of an adverse experience with a product that is reported by an individual, provider or patient, that has not been solicited or not anticipated.

Stability indicating assay: An analytical test of a drug product that can differentiate between the active drug and metabolites.

Stability testing: Evaluation of a product's integrity and absence of degradation of active ingredients (minimal) based on predetermined standards, and performed during clinical studies and commercialization. Stability testing must be done with identical packaging to clinical and/or commercial packaging. The FDA provides a guidance document for drug substance and drug product stability requirements. For marketing and shelf-life needs, it is desirable to have at least a two year expiration date for commercial products. Stability and compatibility in different diluents for parenteral products (e.g., normal saline, dextrose in water) is required. Examination of temperature extremes (e.g., accelerated conditions, freeze-thaw, and humidity) needs to be done also.

Stable disease (SD): Cessation of progression in the disease pathology, physical size, or signs and symptoms of disease, but the disease remains present at its original extent.

Standard deviation (SD): The calculation of the distribution of values for a parameter being studied around an average value that can be, for example, 95% of the variation for one standard deviation.

Standard Letter: Written responses for medical information inquiries from customers (providers or patients) that are prepared in advance for commonly received questions.

Standard operating procedures (SOP): A written, detailed, required set of actions and responsibilities for performing a function to achieve uniformity in performance.

Statistically significant: Describes a mathematical measure of difference between groups. The difference is said to be statistically significant if it is greater than what might be expected to happen by chance alone 95% of the time. Although statistically significance usually refers to the 95% confidence level, sometimes other confidence levels such as higher at 99% or lower at 90% are specified.

Statistical report: Report of the study outcomes using the associated predetermined statistical methods used to generate and analyze data, plus all the results and analyses, often in tabular or graphic forms, along with comments about the statistical significance of the data and outcomes. It is integrated into a final clinical study report.

Steady state concentration: The sustained amount of a product in the plasma or bloodstream, expressed as a concentration or product level, following repeated standard dosing.

Sterile water for injection (SWI): Water used for dilution and preparation of injectable products that is "sterile," free of any microbial contamination through a sterilization process.

Sterility: The property of a product that indicates the absence of contaminating micro-organisms in the formulation.

Stockholder: A person or institution that owns shares of stock in a company.

Stock options: A contractual right to buy shares of a specific stock at a predetermined price (strike price). Often, they are provided to employees as a form of incentive compensation, based on an expectation of rising value of the stock, and based on certain levels of performance of the company and the individual.

Strategic national stockpile: Medical counter-measures for counterterrorism maintained by the federal government, for example, antidotes, vaccines, and antibiotics, especially for microbial, nuclear, and poisonous attacks.

Strength, weakness, opportunity, and threat (SWOT): An analysis of a program or product that considers the four aforementioned traits, often used for marketing or research planning, to avoid or minimize the negative traits of weakness and threats and maximize the positive traits of strength and opportunity.

Strike price: (1) The target exercise price for stock options. (2) Also and differently, the price of a drug set for a specific purpose, as in the initial drug pricing at its first approval or a price resulting from a negotiation between a payer and a manufacturer.

Structure activity relationship (SAR): The chemical structure of a molecule is assessed for the beneficial and adverse actions based on its components (moieties within the structure) and their relative contribution to the overall or specific effects.

Structure based design: The creation of molecules based on the specific substructures that could comprise a molecule with each offering potential added properties from the substructure to the overall molecule, realizing that the overall activity of the molecule is a composite of these individual and interacting activities.

Structured product labeling (SPL): FDA requirement for new drug application labeling using XML software system.

Study completion date: The calendar date when the last patient has been admitted to the study, and all study requirements are completed for all patients. The study is closed.

Study coordinator: A person who is responsible for all the activities and records for a study at a site or group of sites.

Study initiation date: The calendar date when a study enrolls the first patient to be screened for admission into the study.

Subacute toxicity: The study of the toxic and adverse effects of a product usually over 7–14 days, or to up to 90 days, of use usually in animals.

Subcutaneous (SC): The administration of an injectable product through and under the skin and into the tissue, but not deep enough to reach muscle.

Sub-investigator: An investigator at one site in a multi-center clinical study who is responsible for patient safety and conduct of the study at their site, but is not the principal investigator and works under the guidance of the principal investigator.

Substrate: A compound or product that is acted upon by other compounds in a biologic system, for example, the product being metabolized by enzymes in the liver.

Subject: A healthy person or one with a specific target disease who agrees to participate in a study and who will receive the test or control article in the study, as well as any other tests indicated in the study protocol.

Subject matter: In patents, this is the category in which the invention fits.

Summary basis of approval (SBA): The document that presents the information used by the FDA in the approval of a product for marketing.

Superiority study: A study that is intended to disprove the null hypothesis by showing that the groups are different. Placebo control is used for a comparison to determine if something is better than nothing. Active control (mano y mano) is used for a comparison to show one therapy is better than another.

Supplemental new drug application (SNDA): A submission to the FDA to obtain a change in a product or its labeling, usually for a new indication, a new dose, more adverse effect information, reduction in a limitation, relaxation of a specification, new analytical methods, change in the manufacture, use of a different contractor in manufacture or labeling or packaging, or a new formulation or addition of imprinting code.

Supplemental patent certificate (SPC): Under the patent term restoration sections of the Hatch-Waxman Act (1994), a patent which claims a human drug product, medical device, food or color additive first approved for marketing after September 24, 1984 may qualify for patent term extension, as determined by the Patent and Trademark Office with support from the FDA. Regardless of whether the patent claims a product, a method of using a product, or a method of manufacturing a product, the applicant for a patent term extension must establish that: (1) the patent has not expired, (2) the patent has never been extended, (3) the application for extension is submitted by the owner of record of the patent or its agent and includes details relating to the patent and regulatory review time spent in securing FDA approval, (4) the product has been subject to a regulatory review period within the meaning before its commercial marketing or use, (5) the approval: (A) is the first permitted commercial marketing or use of the product, or (B) in the case of products manufactured using recombinant DNA technology, it is the first permitted commercial marketing or use of a product manufactured under the process claimed in the patent, and (6) the application for extension of the term of the patent was submitted to Patent and Trademark Office within 60 days of FDA approval of the commercial marketing application.

Supply chain: The companies and groups involved in sequential distribution of a product, including, for example, at least and in order, manufacturer, wholesaler, retailer, and consumer.

Surrogate endpoints: Study parameters for a disease under investigation that are not direct measures of the disease, but are representative of disease changes and drug action and demonstrate efficacy of a product and a disease's final clinical endpoints, that is, cholesterol levels in blood and thromboembolic events in acute myocardial infarction.

Surveillance, Epidemiology, and End Results (SEER): This program of the National Cancer Institute is a collection of central cancer registries in the United States that collect and submit cancer incidence, prevalence, mortality, survival, stage at diagnosis data and other statistics to the National Cancer Institute. The National Cancer Act of 1971 mandated the collection, analysis, and dissemination of data useful in the prevention, diagnosis, and treatment of cancer leading to the establishment of the SEER Program. Cancer incidence and survival statistics are available from 1973, the first year SEER began collecting data, up to the most recent year for which data are reported. SEER collects data from 18 population-based registries throughout the United States, so incidence and survival statistics are available for just those covered areas, which comprise more than 25 percent of the U.S. population. Mortality data provided by the National Center for Health Statistics, and population data obtained from the Census Bureau, are also available. The publications available on this site include annual reports of the most recent cancer statistics used to track trends over time, topical statistical monographs, and coding and staging manuals for cancer registrars.

Suspected adverse experience: An adverse clinical or laboratory experience by a patient during the use of a product that may be attributed to the product, but the cause–effect relationship has not yet been established.

Sustained release: Delivery of a product gradually over time from a formulation into the patient.

Symptoms, objective findings, assessment, and plan (SOAP): In a healthcare setting, the healthcare provider assesses a patient and determines their care based on a simple organized process, including documentation of symptoms (patient complaints) and objective findings (e.g., lab tests, physical signs observed, or disease signs observed), followed by assessment of this disease and patient presentation, along with preliminary judgments being offered, and then completed at this point in time with the plans of actions being specified for the patient, such as future tests to be done and treatments of any kind, often along with timeframes for all the follow-up work and follow-up expected, but potential, outcomes to be achieved.

T

Takeaway: The core message or information in advertising, a sales call, lecture, or any discussion that you want the recipients to remember.

Target: An in vivo protein (ligand), enzyme, receptor, signaling protein or other molecule that may play a pathologic role in particular disease process and could be altered by drug or biological products to ameliorate the disease.

Targeted medicine: The use of genomic data in patient care that identifies differences in patients' drug response profiles and predicts the best possible treatment options.

Target identification: Process by which potential disease targets are investigated, screened, and prioritized. It involves a detailed knowledge of the normal physiology and disease processes at a molecular level.

Target plasma concentration: Defined as an effective concentration of a drug in the plasma in animal or human studies that will produce a desired effect.

Target product profile (TPP): The desired set of characteristics of a product for its intended use that represent the ideal outcomes that may be achieved during the development of a product. Efficacy outcomes (specific endpoints and degrees of improvement), adverse events, dosage and administration, manufacturing benefits or limits, formulation, regulatory hurdles, and competition comprise the main characteristics in the target product profile. Novelty, competitive advantage, unmet patient needs, costs of goods, and premium pricing are key drivers in setting the target product profile.

Target validation: Process by which the role that a target plays in a disease is fully characterized and established. A combination of in vitro and in vivo functional studies is done. Common tools are cellular-based assays, antisense, RNAi, and knockout mice.

Teams: A group of individuals charged with a specific responsibility, be that a specific study, market, product, or program, who must communicate, delegate, and collaborate effectively performing their work individually and collectively with the expectation of higher efficiency and accountability than could be achieved individually, in order to achieve the overall desired outcomes.

Test article: The product, device or other article that is being evaluated in a study.

Test article accountability: The forms, process, and systems for keeping track of a product under evaluation in a study or test procedure.

Testing facility: The physical building where the study or examination of a product is being done.

Test system: The construct (equipment, processes, and people) that is used to evaluate a product.

Therapeutic equivalence (TE): (1) Drug products classified as therapeutically equivalent can be substituted with the full expectation that the substituted product will produce the same clinical effect and safety profile as the prescribed product. Drug products are considered to be therapeutically equivalent only if they meet these criteria: They are pharmaceutical equivalents (contain the same active ingredient(s), dosage form and route of administration, and strength) and they are assigned by FDA the same therapeutic equivalence codes starting with the letter "A." To receive a letter "A," the FDA designates a brand name drug or a generic drug to be the Reference Listed Drug. (2) Two drugs from different pharmacologic classes can be considered therapeutically equivalent by providers at healthcare institutions if they produce the same or very similar changes in disease pathogenesis and desired disease outcomes. Publications in refereed medical journals of clinical trials conducted with the same study designs must establish this equivalence.

Therapeutic index (TI): Regarding dosing of pharmaceuticals, the difference between the lowest effective dose and the lowest acceptable toxic dose.

Therapeutic window: Regarding dosing of pharmaceuticals, the difference between the lowest effective drug concentration and the lowest acceptable toxic drug concentration in the blood.

Thought-leader (TL): Influencer of current medical practice, research, or education, who is often capable of inspiring peers to improve patient outcomes through his or her research excellence, scientific literature credentials, clinical expertise, and esteemed position and affiliated institution for his or her place of work.

Tiered formulary: A drug list subdivided into levels based on different diagnostic and therapeutic criteria or based on brand drugs versus generic drugs, and associated different co-pays by the patient for patient access to the drugs.

Time and events schedule (T&E): The various specified major activities (events) and their predetermined timeframes collected together and integrated into one plan (schedule) to achieve some predetermined goal.

Time to maximum concentration: The amount of time required following administration of a product to achieve the highest product concentration in the plasma, blood, or other biologic fluid.

Time to progression (TTP): The amount of time required for a disease to significantly progress to the next and more serious stage of disease.

Title XVIII: Social Security Act (1965).

Title XIX: Medicare legislation.

Toxicokinetics: The correlation of pharmacokinetic and toxicology studies usually in preclinical studies in animals. Requirements include selecting appropriate animal species for toxicity study (e.g., same metabolites as human and sufficiently high), comparing findings across species (e.g., species-specific toxicity), and relating exposure to toxicity findings (e.g., differentiate lack of toxicity from lack of exposure).

Trademark: A trademark, ™, or ®, is a distinctive sign or word of some kind that is used publicly by an organization to uniquely identify itself, its products, and/or its services to customers, government, and the public, and to distinguish itself from those of other products, services, and organizations. Conventionally, a trademark is composed of a name, word, phrase, logo, symbol, design, image, or a combination of these elements. A trademark is a type of industrial property that is distinct from other forms of intellectual property.

Trade name: The unique name given to a product by the United States Approved Name organization usually based on a specific name request from a company.

Transdermal: The administration of a product or passage of a product across and through the skin and ultimately into the patient's circulation.

Transgenics: (1) The genetic manipulation of an organism by gene addition or deletion ("knock-out") to the organism's genome, in order to create an animal with a new trait, often a disease that can mimic human disease, such that the animal becomes a model for the human disease, in which new drugs can be tested more reliably. (2) An alternative goal of transgenics is the addition of a human gene to an animal such that the animal will produce the desired human protein from the inserted gene. Sheep and cattle can produce human proteins in their milk, which can be harvested and then purified.

Travel and entertainment expenses (T&E): The set of expenses for a trip that involve either travel or entertainment, including meals, costs of social events conducted, lodging, and all travel by any means (air, land, sea, or parking), gratuities, and taxes that were charged for the aforementioned expenses.

Treatment IND: A special investigative new drug application wherein investigational new drugs are made available to desperately ill patients early in drug development process, prior to approval for marketing. Evidence from the sponsor must be provided in the following four areas: preliminary evidence of a drug's efficacy, preliminary evidence of a drug's safety, documentation that the drug is intended to treat a serious or life-threatening disease, and documentation that no alternative therapy is available to treat the intended stage of disease in the target patient population. Patients may not be eligible for enrollment in definitive clinical trials, that usually must be well underway (e.g., during phase 3), if not almost finished.

Trial endpoints: The pre-specified limits for an individual or group of targeted monitoring parameters for a disease for a particular group of patients for a specific study that are the desired outcomes, such as blood pressure reduction or number of patients improved, or undesired outcomes, such as adverse events (number or extent), at the end of the study.

Tufts Center for Drug Development: A university based group affiliated with Tufts University in Boston that tracks, evaluates, and reports on industry and related regulatory activities, including research and development and sales and marketing areas.

Tumor rounds: The periodic review of terminal cancer cases by the faculty and staff at a teaching medical center, in order to teach students, residents, and fellows about the diagnosis, prognosis, therapies, and outcomes in cancer.

U

Unanticipated problems in research subjects: The guidance from Office of Human Research Protections in Health and Human Services considers any incident, experience or outcome an unanticipated problem if it is of an unexpected nature, severity, or frequency given the research procedures described in the institutional review board-approved research protocol, informed consent form or related documents and taking into account the characteristics of the subject population; if it is or may be related (with "reasonable possibility") to participation in the clinical trial; and if it may place trial participants or others at greater risk of physical, psychological, economic or social harm than was previously known or recognized.

Unexpected adverse experience: An adverse experience associated with the use of a product in specificity or severity that is not listed in the investigator's brochure or the labeling, such as the package insert.

Unit: A measurement of the activity of a product (not the actual mg weight) based on an accepted national or international standard for the activity of the type of product in a biological system (e.g., units of insulin for glucose adjustment or units of interferon for antiviral activity).

Unit dosing (UD): Preparation of doses of product for patients, wherein each administration of each dose is prepared separately and ready for use based on the prescribed amount.

United States Approved Names (USAN): The purpose of the United States Approved Names Council is to serve the health professions in the United States by selecting simple, informative, and unique nonproprietary names for drugs by establishing logical nomenclature classifications based on pharmacological and/or chemical relationships. The United States Approved Names Council (tri-sponsored by the American Medical Association, the United States Pharmacopeial Convention, and the American Pharmacists Association) aims for global standardization and unification of drug nomenclature and related rules to ensure that drug information is communicated accurately and unambiguously, working closely with the International Nonproprietary Name Program of the World Health Organization, and various national nomenclature groups.

United States Pharmacopeia (USP): Develops (and publishes the United States Pharmacopeia–National Formulary) public standards to provide quality oversight for FDA-approved drugs and related articles. The standards originate from pharmaceutical manufacturers based on the draft monographs and data they provide. The United States Pharmacopeia's scientific staff and volunteer experts review this input, conduct necessary laboratory tests, and ensure that the information is subject to a process of public review and comment. The public process helps to refine and finalize this information for publication in the United States Pharmacopeia–National Formulary. A United States Pharmacopeia Expert Committee comprised of volunteer scientists elected on the basis of their knowledge and expertise makes the final decisions to publish standards in the United States Pharmacopeia–National Formulary. Regulatory authorities around the world use these standards in their drug regulations to ensure product quality and protect public health.

University Health Systems Consortia (UHC): Formed in 1984, this is an alliance of 97 academic medical centers and 149 of their affiliated hospitals representing nearly 90% of the nation's non-profit academic medical centers. The UHC offers its members specific programs and services to improve clinical, operational and patient safety performance. The mission of the University Health-System Consortium is to advance knowledge, foster collaboration, and promote change to help members succeed in their respective markets. The UHC's vision is to be a catalyst for change, accelerating the achievement of clinical and operational excellence.

Unmet medical need: (1) Lack of effective treatments, or (2) woefully inadequate current therapies (excess toxicity, or inadequate efficacy, or very inconvenient administration), or (3) a large undiagnosed population, or (4) a largely under-treated population.

User fee: A sum of money paid by a company to a regulatory authority as part of the application for approval to market the product. The sum has historically been used to fund staff for the product reviews by the agency. The fees go into the general fund of the agency. User fees were created in the U.S. by the PDUFA laws.

Utility: A statement by a patent applicant describing how a potential product can be used and why it has potential value to humans.

Utilization review: A process for the assessment and documentation of the appropriateness of product usage based on some predetermined set of criteria, usually some national standard.

V

Validation: Formal assessment of a process or system to establish proof of its desired performance, including an analytical test, plan, protocol, and data collected.

Validation, product: A set of parameters addressed in establishing the performance characteristics ("validation") of a product during its research and development process. How well does the product work? How selective is the product for the target? How stable is the product? How long is the product available to patients? Where does the product distribute after administration? What are the toxic effects of the product?

Validation, target: A set of parameters addressed in establishing the performance characteristics ("validation") of a target in the product research process. What does the target do? What role does the target play in the disease? How specific is the target for the disease? When inhibiting a target, is there an impact on the disease? When inhibiting a target, what other effects are there, such as toxicity?

Value: Relative and perceived overall benefit or utility of a product or service to a person, group, or company, based on its activity, benefits, costs, and problems with its use.

Value chain: A series of companies, services, groups, or individuals that work in a serial manner and increase value creating an outcome. Each possesses some benefits and resolve problems for an organization. It may be, for example, a sales process for a product, manufacturing a product, or developing a product in research and development.

Vector: A carrier for a drug or genetic material from one organism to another.

Vendor: Group, company, or individual that possesses some desired expertise and provides services or products to another entity in exchange for compensation.

Venture capital (VC): Financial support from an individual, group, or company for a new company in general or for a specific endeavor, generally at an early stage of their evolution as a company, at a time of relatively high financial risk, and wherein success is possible but uncertain.

Veterans Administration (VA): The U.S. government department that is responsible for the healthcare system for ex-military personnel (veterans), which includes the VA's own hospitals and healthcare institutions, including physical buildings, systems, equipment, and staff, as well as policies and procedures.

Vial: Container system for liquid products especially for injection, usually made of glass or plastic, with a stopper and cap permitting access via a needle to withdraw the medication.

Visual analogue scale (VAS): A measurement of a product's activity in changing a disease parameter as perceived by a patient or a monitor, based on a 10-cm line delineated at each end by the least possible action and the most possible action, and in which the patient visualizes or the monitor ascertains subjectively the response and marks directly on the line this perception of existence or change in the parameter.

Volume of distribution (VD): The calculated amount (space or volume) a product will distribute throughout the body or animal; for example, 5 liters in a human indicates only distribution in the bloodstream, up to 70 liters indicating distribution throughout the body.

Voluntary action indicated (VAI): A regulatory action by the FDA documented in a letter to a company that specifies and requests an action to be taken, but it is not required to be done and is voluntary.

W

Waiver: A request to a regulatory authority by a sponsor to obviate a requirement in the regulations, along with an explanation as to why the sponsor's compliance is unnecessary or cannot be achieved, and a description of alternative submissions or course of action that satisfies the purpose of the requirement.

Warning letters: Written communication from a regulatory agency to a sponsor or manufacturer to correct violations promptly and threatening enforcement action. Letters illustrate specifically what is not acceptable and what must be done as corrective actions.

Water for injection: The fluid (water) to be used to prepare and dilute a product for parenteral administration.

Web-site: The internet site of a company or person wherein they advertise and/or provide information, they can be contacted, products or services can be ordered and purchased, or other services can be provided via the internet systems, affording efficient and cost-effective processes.

Weeds & seeds: Pharmacognosy, the pharmacy discipline for botanic pharmaceuticals.

Wholesale acquisition cost (WAC): The price paid by a wholesaler for drugs purchased from the wholesaler's supplier, typically the manufacturer of the drug. On financial statements, the total of these amounts equals the wholesaler's cost of goods sold. Publicly disclosed or listed wholesale acquisition cost amounts may not reflect all available discounts.

Wholesaler: Any entity to which a manufacturer sells or arranges to sell products, but they do not relabel or repackage the product, and they provide the product to retail outlets or end users of a product.

Women's health initiative: Any healthcare program created and intended to mitigate a health concern specific to women, be it diagnostic, preventive, or treatment in nature.

Working cell bank: The functional parent cells originating from recombinant DNA or monoclonal antibody technologies and responsible for producing human proteins that are stored and used in manufacturing subsequent lots of biologic products.

Written request: FDA document sent to sponsors requesting pediatric studies. Specific information includes indication, population, types of studies, safety, follow-up, and timeframe for response. Requirements for such written requests include a prevalence of 50,000 pediatric patients annually, a meaningful therapeutic benefit for children, and adequate safety already being demonstrated in adults and animals.

X

Xenotransplantation: An organ, tissue sample, or cell sample from one species given to another species to correct a functional deficiency.

Y

Yield: In product manufacturing, the amount of desired material produced in a manufacturing lot.

10K: An annual report required by the Securities and Exchange Commission (SEC) that contains a comprehensive overview of a public company's business.

10Q: A quarterly report required by the SEC for public companies.

21 CFR 314.5: Section of the Code of Federal Regulations dealing with New Drug Application.

21 CFR part 601: Section of the Code of Federal Regulations dealing with Biologics License Application.

21 CFR 314.94: Section of the Code of Federal Regulations dealing with Abbreviated New Drug Application.

90-Day conference: Within 90 days of filing a new drug application, biologics license application, or investigational device exemption, the Center for Drug Evaluations and Research allows a meeting to occur between the sponsor and the FDA reviewers and officials to discuss the NDA/BLA/IDE and any deficiencies or questions from the FDA.

356h FDA Form: FDA form for the sponsor to apply to market a new drug, biologic, or an antibiotic for human use.

483 Form: FDA form dealing with observations during their inspections conducted with the sponsor.

505(b)(2): Abbreviated new drug application, usually for generic drug approvals with different dosage or rate of absorption established, but without bioequivalence required for a new product that can be considered interchangeable with the branded drug.

505(j): Abbreviated new drug application for generic versions of a branded drug, requiring proof that it is the same drug and bioequivalent, with new safety and effectiveness data not required. Products are considered interchangeable.

510 (k): Device application with FDA.

1571 FDA Form: FDA form for adverse event reporting.

1572 FDA Form: FDA form for the principal investigator in a study to complete.

3397: FDA form for user fees.

3500: FDA form for safety information and adverse experience reporting (Medwatch).